# GETTING READY to READ

# GETTING READY to READ

Prepared by the

### BANK STREET COLLEGE
*of* EDUCATION

## Betty Doyle Boegehold
AUTHOR

### DR. CLAUDIA LEWIS
CONSULTANT

### WILLIAM H. HOOKS
SERIES EDITOR

BALLANTINE BOOKS · NEW YORK

Library of Congress Catalog Card Number: 83-91160
ISBN 0-345-30519-1

Manufactured in the United States of America
First Edition: April 1984
10 9 8 7 6 5 4 3 2 1

# Contents

# EXPANDED CONTENTS

CHAPTER 5
*FROM "ME" TO "YOU AND ME":*
*FOUR- AND FIVE-YEAR OLDS*

CHAPTER 8
## THE BEGINNING OF SCHOOL—AND AFTER

# Foreword

Reading the words in a book! I can dimly recall my joy in this mastery, and even see faintly in my mind's eye that little Victorian primer that was my first book. Much easier to recall, and with even a more vivid delight, are the hours when my mother read aloud to me and my three brothers and sister. I think the first books were the Beatrix Potter stories of Peter Rabbit and Benjamin Bunny, as well as the tale of "The Three Little Kittens Who Lost Their Mittens," and, a little later, when we were sturdy enough for such fairy tales, the dreaded but adored story of "Rumpelstiltskin." As we grew into our school years and our interests expanded, we were treated not only to the Old Testament Bible stories but to the then very popular adventures of Paul Du Chaillu in Africa and in the Land of the Long Night. How we shuddered pleasurably over the thought of eating snake soup in the jungles of Africa! Even as we grew into the junior high years the reading aloud continued, and I treasure the memory of all of us sitting on the porch stairs, listening to Dickens' *Great Expectations*.

I became an avid reader myself at a fairly early age, and all my associations with reading have been happy ones throughout my life. This is not so for countless children, of course. We are all familiar with the picture of reading badly begun and never really mastered; reading the great stumbling block leading straight to school failure.

The possible reasons for this have filled many a book—as indeed they should, since there is no one way to account for a hatred and fear of reading.

One of the most common mistakes we make is to try to introduce reading to a child long before he or she is ready for it, physiologically, emotionally, intellectually. Some children pick it up as early as age four or five; others—even though they may become college professors when they grow up—cannot turn to reading with any ease at all until seven or eight. Readiness differs, as do home environments, cultural surroundings, and a multitude of both physiological and psychological factors. Pushing the child toward what is for him or her an incomprehensible and inappropriate task is one of the surest ways to implant deep-seated trouble around every aspect of what should be the pleasurable process of learning to read.

Betty Boegehold's book on the pre-reading period in children's lives shows us what a rich time of preparation it can be and should be for every child from infancy through the toddler stage and preschool years right up to age six and formal school entry. Yes, there are specific ways to prepare infants for future reading! *Getting Ready to Read* is full of practical suggestions for parents about the informal games, activities, and experiences that lay the necessary foundations for reading. It also offers a most welcome, highly readable framework of knowledge and information about reading readiness as related to the developmental stages of childhood.

Moreover, there is ample discussion of ways of furthering the language and concept development so important for the young learner if he or she is to read with real understanding. For reading is not a matter of simply decoding those black marks on the page and turning them into words. It is a matter of drawing from the words meaning that can be related to what one has experienced or come to know in some personal, vital way. The grasp of concepts—that is, seeing basic relationships and discovering concrete meanings behind words—contributes to the young child's ability to read; that process enriches reading at any stage of life.

The stages of childhood overlap; that is, what is experienced or learned in the earliest years carries over and extends with variations into later stages. There is a continuum in development. For this reason, the reader should not expect to find here a how-to book to be read piecemeal for what it has to say about the specific years of infancy, toddlerhood, etc. Rather, it is a book to pursue throughout for a better understanding of the movement and flow of development and readiness in childhood.

Among the book's practical suggestions, certainly one of the most useful will be the help offered in spotting those cues that are indicators of readiness to read. For the whole matter is such an individual one. The right time for one child may not be the right time for another of the same age and apparently similar physical characteristics. Respect for the individual child and his or her pattern of development is at the core for promoting success in reading. And indeed, an underlying respect for individual—mother, father, child—illuminates every lively page of this helpful book, one that can be enjoyed while it is at the same time offering first aid on a score of problems and practical issues.

—Claudia Lewis, Ph.D.

# ACKNOWLEDGMENTS

Grateful acknowledgment is made to Joëlle Delbourgo for her role in conceptualizing this series; to Pat Ayres for bringing Bank Street and Ballantine Books together; to Dr. Richard Ruopp, President of Bank Street College; to the many faculty members who supported this project; and to Mary Fitzpatrick, Joan Auclair, and Pat Rogers for manuscript preparation.

Gratitude is also acknowledged to Amy Dombro, Director of the Infant and Family Center at Bank Street College for allowing the author access to her group, and for critiquing this manuscript; to Pearl Zeitz and to Ann Welborn of the Bank Street School for Children for their help in supplying samples of reading testing materials; to Paul Schwarz and David Wolkenberg for the chance to observe their classrooms; and to my granddaughter, Julie Simon, for providing a living example of how to raise a reading child.

# GETTING READY to READ

# Introduction: Why Read?

## THE NEED TO READ

Why should we prepare our children to become successful readers? In the video-computer world of the near future, who will be reading? Will our children still need to read and to enjoy books?

The answer is: yes! Success in school—and later in life—still depends on the ability to read competently. To fully comprehend math, social studies, foreign languages, science, or computer interaction, children have to master reading first. They must not only decode words, but understand instructions and questions. No matter how much we use—or will use—visual and push-button teaching techniques, these methods still rely on comprehension of a written language. Those who can read and understand the records of our past will be less likely to repeat past errors and, we hope, may create new solutions to old problems. Literate young people will be the leaders of the future. Thus, a child without good reading skills will be a deprived child—deprived of a major asset for success in the adult world.

---

## THE POWER OF READING

Reading is power: power to grasp the many facets of a business venture; power to understand the actions of a government that affects our daily activities; power to affect that government ourselves by our own use of words.

But, to me, the greatest power of reading is the effect it has on our personal lives. Good readers can search the past for answers, learn about the world around us, probe people's guesses about the future, or soar on the wings of fantasy. Reading can change us: our personal opinions, our way of thinking, our political views, even our actions—all can be influenced by our reading.

Of course, we are affected, too, by the vividness of the world that TV represents. But TV images change so fast; people fall, ships crash, wars begin—all in a few winks of the eye. And we can't stop and ponder their meaning or hold the pictures still while we grasp their import. We seldom see a subject explored in depth; the limits of time control the pictures. To know more, we must read more.

## THE FIRST STEP TO READING

In the last decade, reading scores have plummeted; presidents, distinguished panels, educators, and laypeople have rushed to fill the air waves and printed pages with programs for correcting this alarming drop in literacy.

Concerned parents may feel bewildered by the various panaceas offered on all sides. Should they

- return to basics (however *basics* may be interpreted)?
- teach two-year-olds to read?
- start school at three?
- even begin teaching while a child is in the womb?

A great deal of nonsense has been offered as a solution, some of it harmless, but some of it dangerous. Why? Because following some of the proffered plans, while initially producing a parrotlike response, tends in the long run to lower, not raise, reading achievement. Another reason for the continued drop in reading scores as a child progresses through school?

The total reasons for the overall decline in reading ability depend on a great many factors: the school's programs and philosophies, the family support system, the makeup, background, and interests of the student body and teacher, group pressures from many sides—all have contributed to the national decline.

You, as a parent, may feel unable to effect much change in this overall problem, but you *can* help your own child to achieve reading success. The premise of Bank Street College is that, after years of research into how children learn, the best and most rewarding method of insuring long-lasting reading success is the enrichment of the preschool child's learning life. In other words, reading readiness is the way to go—and you're the one to do it!

## WHY IS READING READINESS SO IMPORTANT?

*Question*: I don't get it. If reading is important, why don't we teach young children to read as soon as possible?

*Answer*: It can be bad for them, and it doesn't work. Preparing children to read is a more important first step than the actual teaching of reading itself.

*Question*: Why?

*Answer*: That's the purpose of this book. To discuss all the ways of pre-reading preparation that parents can practice, and why they should do it. Why teaching preschoolers to read is not a good idea. Why a holistic reading readiness preparation actually produces better readers. And what fun it can be.

*Question*: My friend's four-year-old daughter taught herself a lot of words. So why shouldn't her mother teach her more?

*Answer*: "Taught herself"—that's the key phrase. The child did it herself from her own needs and curiosity. Mama can help when asked, but otherwise, hands strictly off.

*Question*: Why?

*Answer*: Read this book and you'll find out. But here's an overview of some of our basic reasons.

As you probably know, there are two essential parts to reading, which educators call *decoding* and *comprehension*. *Decoding* means figuring out what the letters and words *are*. In other words, decoding is the ability to look at the printed page and decipher the words, phrases, and sentences. *Comprehension* is what the letters and words *mean*. Comprehension is the ability to understand what concepts and images the words convey, what information they are giving, what feelings they arouse, what beauty or despair they illuminate.

It is easier to decode than to comprehend. Decoding is a necessary but a learned rote skill, one that can be learned in a series of planned steps for most children. But comprehension requires far more subtle skills. It requires a child to be exposed to rich experiences, usually by a guiding adult hand; a child that has been encouraged to question, to experiment, to test, to make judgments, evaluations, and conclusions, right or wrong. It requires a child with skills to approach new experiences with confidence and eagerness; and, above all, a child who has been "bathed" in language, who has been familiar with books and stories from crib days. Such a child brings a richness of understanding to what words mean, and is physically, emotionally, mentally, and socially—in other words, developmentally—ready to read successfully.

## WHAT THE RESEARCH REVEALS

But what about that nagging feeling that your child may be missing out on something very important, if you don't teach him to decode as early as possible?

Studies of the long-term advantages for children who have been forced to read at an early age do not show good results. They may show an initial advantage, but the well-prepared child soon not only catches up to them, but outdistances them. There is strong evidence that those children who are taught to read before they are school age become indifferent readers—those who read from necessity rather than with pleasure. And most important of all, according to many noted child psychologists, it is the child who has a long, rich reading readiness preparation that becomes the eager and independent reader.

Studies conducted by the New York City Board of Education show that five-year-old children who were taught to read lost almost all of their reading skills over the summer vacation. Further findings showed that children who got formal reading instruction before they were six were less likely to enjoy reading than those who began later. One of the few long-term reading research projects that followed a group of children from school entry through junior high school was conducted by the famed educator Carleton Washburn. The observers found that the adolescents who had been introduced to formal reading later than first grade were more enthusiastic spontaneous readers than those who began to read in first grade. (In Scandinavia and Russia, too, reading isn't taught until age seven.) Eager spontaneous readers in post-elementary years are not only going to make better use of high school and college opportunities, but will be far better prepared for job opportunities in later life.

The titles of several highly respected books that agree with this "later reading" approach reflect the concern of the authors about the rush to teach preschoolers skills they are not developmentally prepared to master. *The Hurried Child*, by David Elkind; *Don't Push Your Preschooler*, by Louise Bates Ames and Joan Ames Chase; and *Don't Push Me, I'm No Computer*, by Helen L. Beck, all agree with this premise.

The child who reads when he is totally prepared to read establishes a habit that lasts throughout his schooling and beyond. The child who was made to read, or never given a rich reading background, only reads when she has to, and does not become a life-long book reader. So keep your eye on the positive long-term values as you enjoy working with your child in the present.

## THE FIRST AND BEST TEACHER

Another important factor in our insistence that "good reading readiness" is more important than the actual teaching of reading, is that the child's first teacher—you—is already equipped to provide the best reading readiness. For most parents, generation after generation, do provide such preparation even without knowing it. You probably have already begun to do so. Our aim is to make you more aware of the variety of activities that provide the best preparation, so that you will more consciously understand and plan for the kind of materials and guidance this book suggests.

And we also promise that you will have fun doing so— you and your child will both enjoy the benefits of this approach. Best of all, we assure you that this approach works!

So relax. Don't join the rush to short-change children by overstructuring their first years with attempts to teach them the mechanics of reading. (Even those few children who teach themselves to decode words at an early age need the same kind of readiness experiences as other children.) We need to do what is appropriate for each of the developmental stages of childhood. Yes, there are lots of things that parents can do with the infant, the toddler, and the preschooler to prepare them for reading. For each stage there are specific activities that contribute to reading readiness, and parents are the best qualified to provide them. The premise of this book is that the preschool years of childhood should be a period of rich reading readiness; the more lasting promise is that your child will become not only a reader, but an eager, successful reader.

# CHAPTER
# 1

# *Parent Modeling*

Parents are the most important models in a young child's life, and parents' actions and attitudes have a powerful effect on their young ones. I'm using the word *parents* to mean the person or persons who care for the child. This could be one or two natural parents, a grandparent, a stepparent, a foster parent, or any older person who is the primary caregiver.

In times past, parents might have said, "Do as I say, not as I do," but this doesn't work now—if it ever did! The way we parents act is what the children see; the way we talk is what they hear; they take their cues from us. If we are loving and considerate, the children will believe that is the proper way to act. But what if we are abusive to others or to our children? What if we yell, complain a lot, or don't want to hear what the children are saying? What "modeling" do our children have then?

Let's look at our modeling role as it applies to preparing our children to read. In this case, our own reading activities will carry a lot of meaning to the children. Do we read often? Do we place a lot of value on being able to read? We must be our own judges.

## IMPORTANCE OF PARENTAL READING HABITS

Statistics show that parents who read a lot probably will have children who like to read, too. However, the process isn't as simple as it sounds. The good reading habit isn't caught as easily as the common cold, and it doesn't rub off on children by physical contact. When we look more closely at this process, we'll see that some very concrete actions are involved. Even parents who are themselves hooked on books realize they did more than proclaim their love of reading. Take the Altons, for example. Let's hear their experiences in their own words.

### HOOKED ON BOOKS

*The Altons*, parents of four—two boys and two girls:
*Nora Alton*:
As a kid, I was a hungry reader. I still am! I read the news, novels, how-to books, anything. I read to the children as soon as they were old enough to listen. Before that I told them nursery rhymes, made-up jingles, counting games— you know, like "This little piggy went to the market."

Each kid loved books, but in different ways. Liz only wanted to hear two books for a long time. But Tony wanted different stories all the time. Usually I read or told stories in the morning before we got going. I'm a lazy starter. Sure, sometimes I felt it was a pain in the neck, but most times I enjoyed it.

*Henry Alton*:
I read a lot, but mostly in my field—I'm a biologist. But I enjoy travel books, science fiction, biographies when I want a change. And a good national newspaper. I really enjoy reading to the children. They are great listeners and make such good comments. Kids tell you a lot about how they think.

I try to make a habit of taking the kids to the library. They pick out their books while I'm getting mine. Sometimes the little ones choose stuff that makes me shudder, but it's their choice. We always take a few better books with us, too.

One more thing: now I often see the older kids reading to the younger ones. Isn't that great?

Obviously, the older Alton children have no trouble reading. Their school reports show that they do fairly well in spelling and writing also. They write stories and plays at home, too, and know how to use the dictionary for help. And chances are that the younger children will master reading skills as easily as their siblings did.

Why? Because their parents care about reading, read themselves, and read to their children. Most important of all, Mr. and Mrs. Alton have shared not only books, but their respect and love for books with their children—perhaps the best reason for their children's later success in reading.

## NOT SO HOOKED ON BOOKS

But what about other parents? Those who read books only occasionally, or those whose reading material consists of the daily paper and/or a magazine now and then? Does this mean their children will not be prepared for reading? No. Fortunately, the human race is full of surprises. Children from non-reading homes can and often do become good readers. But the chances are that many children who are not familiar with books or "told" stories will have more difficulty learning to read than other children.

Is there anything that non-reading parents can do to help their children prepare for formal reading? Of course there is.

*Jane Burns*, a single working parent with two small children: I just didn't have time to read myself. Oh, maybe the editorials in the morning paper on the way to work or a magazine article when I was waiting for someone. I tried to read at night, but I always fell asleep—I was so tired! But I knew the kids wanted and needed stories, so I began to read to them every night, even if only for a few minutes. I made it a rule: just like tooth-brushing, story time became part of our nightly ritual.

You know what happened? I really began to enjoy story time, too! I found myself relaxing, nerve by nerve. I could enjoy the kids' enjoyment. Now story time is a really loving time together.

*Maurice Zdenaky*, father of three boys:
Sports are my game. I'm an active guy, always on the go. I take my older kid to games, play ball, skate with the younger ones. So I don't have much time for reading. I'd rather watch television. I haven't read to the kids much, but I like to tell them stories—tall tales, I guess you'd call them. I make up all these way-out adventures I've had, like beating Babe Ruth's record, or escaping from hungry alligators in the Okefenokee. The kids love them. And when I get tired, the kids tell *me* stories.

What else do I do to help the kids get ready to read? Well, I help them figure out signs, players' names, stuff like that. And I answer questions. Sometimes they drive me a little nuts, but how else are they going to learn?

*Cheryll Dakers*, mother of six—four boys and two girls:
I never was much of a reader, but I want my kids to be! I don't have much time to read books to them myself, but I see to it that somebody does—their father or their grandmother. And now the older kids read to the little ones every day. I found out that just knowing their ABC's or numbers wasn't enough—they need to be talked to, sung to. I'm a pretty good singer. We all sing when we're working together—washing dishes, times like that.

And I encourage the kids to put on plays for each other, puppet shows, acting out stories. They sure love to act! Now the older kids are writing plays for school. I'm proud about that!"

These three parents are not great readers, but they share a common concern. They want their children to read. They are really making efforts toward this end and, in fact, are doing a good job.

What important steps are they taking? Jane Burns reads to her children each night; Maurice Zdenaky tells stories and encourages his children to tell their own stories and to figure out words; and Cheryll Dakers sings with her children and encourages their dramatic expression. These various parental actions are important basic pre-reading activities:

- reading aloud and telling stories to children
- helping children to decode signs they see around them
- encouraging children to tell and dramatize stories themselves.

All these steps can be taken by any parent, whether or not he or she is a constant reader. But the *best* preparation requires a little more—it requires parents to get into the act, too!

## READING CHECKLIST

Getting into the act means that parents should take a serious look at their own reading habits and see what they think of them. As a starter, check yourself with this list of questions:

1. What do I read most often?
   A. Newspapers
      - front-page news
      - editorials
      - magazine section
      - sports page
      - other
   B. Magazines
      - articles
      - stories
      - home care
      - gossip columns
      - other
   C. Books: Fiction
      - best-sellers
      - romance
      - mysteries
      - science fiction
      - other

  D. Books: Nonfiction
   · biography
   · travel
   · information
   · how-to
   · other
 2. How often do I read?
   · daily
   · weekly
   · frequently
   · seldom
   · never
 3. Why do I read?
   · to learn the news
   · to find out what other people are doing
   · for pleasure and/or escape
   · to learn something new or how to do something
   · to pass the time
 4. What do I enjoy the most? (Be honest—if you like cartoons or gossip columns or steamy stories, say so, to yourself. It's a clue to expanding your reading along similar themes.)

Now that you know what and when you read, you can make some choices for further reading. Look in the library or bookstore for the kinds of books you think you'll enjoy. For instance, if you like romances, try Daphne DuMaurier's *Rebecca*. If you like lighthearted mysteries, try a book like Elizabeth Peter's *The Camelot Caper*. If you prefer real adventures, Thor Heyerdahl's *Kon Tiki* or *Ra II* could be for you. The point is not to make reading a chore, but a pleasure for you. For your children to see you frequently reading is probably the best message you can give them about the importance—and the fun—of reading.

———

## THE AMAZING BOOK

What advantages there are in having a good book at hand! The histories of countries or of individual people, adventures on the high seas and towering mountains, journeys into the long-ago past or the far-ahead future all await the person setting out to develop new adventures in reading. Books, unlike television, can be carried with you to be read and reread. Unlike television, a book permits you to stop at any point to ponder its message or to attend to other business. A book is always ready for use for as long or as little time as you wish, and you never lose any of the story.

Books are our "gifts from the dead." In them lies the whole of human history, of human strivings to communicate individual beliefs, longings, and knowledge. In spite of our electronic communicators, people who don't read are, in one sense, enchained. They are cut off from these gifts bequeathed by the present as well as the past, and they may be passing these chains down to their children. As one of our elder wise men, the psychoanalyst Bruno Bettelheim, says, "It's not enough that the parents read; they must enjoy it as well. If parents don't enjoy reading or say what was gained from it, children may learn to read signs or labels and ads on television, but they do not grow into literate persons—that is, they never find reading meaningful or gain important values from reading."

And as another wise man, Roger Bacon, said, "Reading maketh a full man." Reading, unlike the swift, undemanding images of television, requires some effort, but the rewards are great.

So how about giving reading an important place in your daily activities? As food nourishes your body, reading will stretch and enlarge your ideas. As sports develop your body, reading develops your mind. What's more, it's fun! And best of all, you will be passing on to your children a greater gift than the most expensive toys: a desire for and love of reading.

## SETTING THE HOME SCENE

So you'll be reading for your own pleasure now. And you will be more involved in setting up a pre-reading program for your kids. What will the home scene look like, as you plan good pre-reading experiences for them?

First, you will have reading material around—paperback or hardcover books, magazines, either bought or borrowed from the library. And there will be children's books available to your offspring. Your books and the children's will have special places in your home. Few of us have a "library" nowadays; we may not even have room for a bookcase. But we can choose to make at least one shelf, whether under a table, in a cupboard, or hanging on a wall, reserved for books alone. The children's books, too, should have their special place rather than being dumped into a toy chest or mixed up with the children's games. The children will imitate the ways you treat a book. They may grumble a bit but still respond to your insistence on respecting a book: not leaving it on the floor, not leaving it sprawled upside down and open, not letting food or drink drip all over it.

A friend of mine still remembers not only how her father read to his children, but how he handled the book:

> He would hold it carefully, as if it were a living creature. First he would smooth the pages from the middle to the back and to the front. He'd gently rub the book's spine, too, with one finger. And, as he read to us, he'd turn the pages lovingly. I learned to respect a book—any book—from Pa.

## QUALITY BOOKS

Perhaps one reason for the seeming disregard for books shown by so many children is the quality of the books they may be given. Usually these are the books from mass-market outlets, such as the supermarkets, drug, and other big stores. At first glance, these books are quite appealing: bright colors, sturdy bindings, gay little themes. But many of these are flimsy, in manufacture and in quality. The texts may consist of just naming objects or places—a good but limited idea for the toddler. The pictures may offer the child little beyond the bright colors. Small wonder the child soon tires of them.

Of course, some of these mass-market books are better than others: those that are reproductions of old favorites, or nursery rhymes, or counting and concept books. The Random House paperbacks are a fine example of inexpensive but well-done books. We need to look carefully before we buy, asking ourselves questions such as:

- Is the subject matter right for my child's age?
- Are the pictures clear and bright?
- Is the book well made, strong enough to withstand my child's handling?
- Am I comfortable with what the book says or shows? Such as lifestyles portrayed, kinds of children and setting shown? What does it say about men's/women's roles? Do I like the underlying philosophy of the book—what it's really saying?
- Could I stand reading it over and over?

Along with a place to keep the books, it is equally important to have a quiet, well-lighted spot where children can enjoy losing themselves in the wonder, fun, and mystery of looking at and handling books and magazines. Later, this spot may become a cherished refuge for the serious reader.

## USING THE LIBRARY

When you take your children to the library, the older ones will probably want to choose their own books, but the youngest, of course, will need some help. The children's librarian is a good source of knowledge and suggestions and will welcome your interest. Browse around, too. You may find old favorites you want to share with your children or new books to arouse their interest. Your whole family will discover what a pleasurable community resource the library is. And don't forget to take out books for yourself—this is the kind of modeling that really counts with children.

The respect we have for books, the way we keep them and handle them, will demonstrate our high regard for books more than any speech we can make, and, of course, the sight of us reading will make that activity not only a symbol of being "grown up," but a skill highly desired by our children. As Betsy Hearne says in *Choosing Books for Children*, "With adults practicing what they preach, any activity seems contagious. Kids will [read] if you will."

# CHAPTER
# 2

# *Important! Begin With The Baby!*

## TEACHING BABIES TO READ?

You've probably heard glowing accounts of how some parents taught their babies to read at eighteen months! Maybe you felt not only surprised but alarmed—is this what you are supposed to do? Teach reading to your baby? Along with all the diapering, feeding, washing, and changing?

Relax. No eminent authorities on child development would support this project; in fact, they would condemn it. Why? First of all, neither the baby's physical nor mental development is ready for such a specialized skill, and it might actually be damaging to attempt to enforce such procedures. Secondly, babies need to devote all their vigorous energies to the business of growing and developing through first-hand experiences of their world—from sucking, biting, looking, hearing, touching, examining, tasting, crawling, and creeping to taking the first unsteady steps, trying to feed themselves, or place one block on another. So providing a setting (which we'll discuss later) that will give your baby chances to develop these sensory experiences is an important foundation for baby's full development.

Reading, important as it is, is a secondhand, not a firsthand experience. The famous Swiss psychologist Jean Piaget tells us that the toddler's/baby's mental development is in a sensory-motor stage. By this he means that the young child cannot reason beyond what he sees, touches, knows through his senses, and thus can't deal with abstract things such as are involved in the reading process.

## PREPARING BABIES FOR READING

Yet this stage, from the earliest months, is of great importance in reading preparation. What, then, does the concerned parent or caregiver do to help children develop reading readiness?

Communicate! Talk to your baby! Sing to your baby! Cuddle your baby! Tell the baby what you are doing as you go about your daily business.

> Now Daddy is getting Johnny's bath ready. Woosh! Here comes the water! In goes Johnny's yellow tugboat, splish-splash. Is the water too hot? Not hot enough? Daddy puts his elbow in the water—Ouch! TOO HOT! We need more cold water!

Johnny won't understand the words, of course; he may not yet understand the action. But he does respond to Daddy's loving concern and to the warm sharing of companionship that is conveyed by Daddy's voice. All babies need to hear these strong sounds of love. Just as they need to be physically cherished, held, and cuddled, so they need to hear warm, human sounds.

## TEACHING HUMAN SPEECH

Of all the species, humans are the only ones who need to teach their young how to speak. Orphan kittens or dogs will mew or bark with the same variety of meanings as do their adults; but human children will not develop competent adult speech without hearing it from babyhood on. With many parents, talking to their children is a natural activity, but in some families, oral expressions of interest and affection aren't considered important with babies or toddlers.

Yet most experts say that the whole foundation of a child's success in reading, writing, communicating—in other words, success at school—is laid in these earliest years.

Nancy Larrick, a renowned specialist in children's reading, says, "The time to begin (language development) is in baby's first year, certainly by the time he/she is four weeks old." She goes on to say that the best ways to develop each child's aptitude for reading are:

1) through rich experience with oral language, and
2) through continuing pleasure in books, which creates an eagerness to read.

## IMITATION AND REWARD

A rich experience with oral language begins with baby's listening to the adults who become the baby's models for spoken language. V. Thomas Mawhinney, author of *Rewarding Parenthood, Rewarding Childhood*, says the baby learns best through *imitation and reward*. Don't be put off by this formal phrase. What he means by *imitation and reward* is that the delighted response to the baby's first syllables encourages more syllables from the baby.

Perhaps little Penny makes a "da" sound when her father is holding her. "Yes, yes, here's Da!" says the excited, proud Daddy. "Come here, Joan! Penny just said my name. She called me 'Da'!"

Who knows what Penny meant? Or if she was assigning a label to an object—a basic but fairly advanced skill. But the adult's praise, followed by repetition of the syllable, begins the slow development of that necessary skill of attaching names to things. The adult's delight in the baby's gradual accumulation of meaningful sounds, shown by physical cuddling, hand clapping, and oral praise, is the *reward* that encourages the baby's further attempts at *imitation*. Children who are deprived of this interchange do not develop language skills as quickly and efficiently.

## BABY TALK

Most experts advise parents not to repeat too often the charming "baby talk" mispronunciations. Rather, as responsible language modelers, they should use the correct pronunciation in talking to their babies or toddlers.

Babies play a lot with language, and need this play. They don't learn to speak the way adults learn a foreign language. Babies don't know a verb from a noun. At first, they don't even know that words mean anything! When they do make the connection, they need lots of time to experiment. Some words will be real tongue-twisters for them: they don't need to hear us repeating their mistakes, but to hear us saying the words correctly. Not that we'll be rigid about it; after all, they are trying their best. Easy does it, is the best rule—as demonstrated in the following episode:

> When taking a bath Penny splashes the water and says, "Wah-wah." Mother, encouraging her, answers, "Yes, *water*. Penny likes the *water*. Nice, warm *water*." Or again, as Penny stretches toward her teddy bear and calls, "Ba-ba! Ba-ba," Mother says, "Bear! Penny wants her bear. Here's Penny's bear."

The more Mother responds to Penny's beginning attempts to talk, the more Penny will try, and the more Mother says the words correctly, the faster Penny will learn them. But no one will ever tell Penny, "That's wrong! Don't say it that way! Say it like this." Such negative put-downs would discourage Penny's eagerness to try talking. Positive reinforcement helps Penny—and most of us—thrive.

## USING THE FAMILIAR

Nursery rhymes, rhymes you make up, explaining, telling stories, or just plain talking—all or any provide that friendly speech contact that lays the cornerstone for baby's own speech later on. The rhythm of the age-old nursery rhymes also seems to help imprint the lilting rhythms of speech on our human young.

It's hard to say these age-old rhymes in a monotone; even the flattest of voices becomes more lively, even bouncy, when reciting:

> Hey Diddle, Diddle
> The cat and the fiddle
> The cow jumped over the moon.
> The little dog laughed
> To see such sport,
> And the dish ran away with the spoon.

Many nursery and other favorite rhymes, whether chanted or sung, involve physical contact with the baby. Experts tell us that such physical accompaniment is important. It reinforces language rhythms through all the baby's senses. And the touching, patting, and rocking make babies feel loved and cherished in the way they respond to best. Try these old favorites:

This little piggy went to market,
This little piggy stayed home;
This little piggy had roast beef,
This little piggy had none.
And this little piggy cried 'wee wee wee' all the way home.

(Adult touches a different toe as each line is spoken. On the last line, the small toe is lovingly shaken.)

———

Hickory dickory dock
The mouse ran up the clock
The clock struck one
And down he run
Hickory dickory dock.

(Adult runs fingers lightly up baby's body to chin. Adult lightly taps baby's nose, runs fingers down baby's body, and tweaks baby's toes.)

Pat-a-cake, pat-a-cake, baker's man
Bake me a cake as fast as you can
Roll it

(Clap baby's hands lightly together. Rub baby's hands together.

And toss it
And mark it with a 'B'

Lift baby's hands. Lightly trace a B on baby's hand.

And bake it in the oven
For baby and me.

Tuck baby's hands inside the adult's hands.)

Rockabye baby in the treetop.
When the wind blows, the cradle will rock.
When the bough breaks, the cradle will fall,
And down will come baby, cradle and all.

(Rocking back and forth. Rocking up and down. Lifting baby high, then gently bouncing her.)

So let's all feel free to talk, to sing, to chant to our babies, to tell them nursery rhymes, or play little games with them such as Peek-a-Boo, I see you! In Peek-a-boo, we put our hands over our faces, then pull them away as our babies delightedly grin back at us. This game helps babies accept the first short separation from their loving adults.

Then comes the time of response: first baby begins the long, sometimes difficult feat of making syllables that stand for things in his world. "Da," baby says, smiling at Papa. Or "li-li," meaning the lighted lamp. Or "Daw! Daw!" (dog), "Kiwi" (kitty), or "Dah-dah" (Grandpa). And most families respond to their babies' first attempts at speech with exclamatory delight. Thus the baby's first speech efforts are reinforced by human praise, encouraging baby to further attempts.

## THE UNENCOURAGED BABY

The child who isn't talked to is apt to be the child whose first efforts to "name and know" his environment go unnoticed. The unencouraged baby will, no doubt, continue to babble sound, but what incentive is there to turn this into speech? When this child finally does so, as a toddler, he will probably be behind his contemporary who has been using words for a long time.

This same child will, no doubt, encounter another problem soon: his questions may well go unanswered. Reliable research tells us that families who don't speak to their babies are often the ones who don't hear their toddlers' halting questions. Or, hearing them, don't reply. And worst of all, some encourage silence rather than questioning. The "seen but not heard" approach to childhood can be a very damaging one. Luckily, most parents respond to their child's first words and questions. Without overwhelming the child with too much information, parents naturally assume the role of first teacher.

## THE BEGINNINGS OF SPEECH

From the earliest days, the baby has moved constantly, wiggling, stretching, waving and pumping hands and feet. And crying! A cry, the baby's first sound, usually brings Mom or Dad to the cribside.

"What's the matter, sweetie-pie?" the parent asks, picking up and patting the crying baby. "Gas pains? Jimmy is hurting? Mommy (or Daddy) will pat the gas all away. There, there!" (The baby continues to cry.) "Is Jimmy just fretful? Jimmy wants some hugging?" (Kissing, hugging, and rocking the baby.) "Shh, shh, shh. Jimmy wants to sleep. Sleepyhead, sleepyhead, go to sleep." (Parent hums, continues rocking and walking around the room until Jimmy quiets down.)

Look what Jimmy has accomplished by making his one sound! He has communicated his distress successfully to his parents; he has caused his parent to do something about it, receiving positive responses through his senses—being patted, kissed, rocked, and talked to; finally, he has been relieved of an unpleasant condition. Pretty good results for a nonverbal child!

## CAN ATTENTION SPOIL AN INFANT?

There are still some parents who believe that a baby will be spoiled if he gets attention when he cries. Some parents see crying as *only* a selfish, attention-getting device. I'm sure none of us see ourselves in these categories, but perhaps we don't fully realize how much babies gain when their cries are heeded. They learn to trust and to love—two basic emotions essential to the best development. And, far from being spoiled, they are able to move on into independence.

I once heard a remark that impressed me deeply: "Security is having had enough"—enough basic love and care. For small ones, having their needs met is to be loved. A baby whose cries bring no help, no comfort, learns not to trust people. A baby whose cries go unanswered often becomes the anxious toddler, constantly demanding responses—even negative ones—from adults. For instance, look at Larry Rogers:

In the playground, two-year-old Larry stood close by his mother, one hand clamped onto the edge of her jacket. The thumb of his other hand was firmly thrust in his mouth. "Go play with the boys and girls," Mrs. Rogers said irritably, pulling her jacket away. "Don't hang on Mommy." Larry took a few steps toward the children. But soon he was back by Mrs. Rogers, clutching at her jacket again. "He's driving me crazy," Mrs. Rogers said. "Always whining, hanging on me, calling me constantly to come to his crib. I tell him he's a big boy now, he's got to stop acting like a baby. I never babied him; I don't know why he's acting so babyish now."

Perhaps poor Larry is still trying for that comforting that was his due as a baby: he hasn't had enough security to move on from babyhood needs. Such needs may well affect his whole development, including his preparation for the important job of reading.

## THE BABBLING BABY

Babies soon begin to babble and coo as well as cry. Many language specialists say that every child everywhere makes the same kind of nondescript babbling sounds. Then the babbling noises begin to take on special notes: French sounds for French babies, Spanish sounds for Spanish babies, Dutch sounds for Dutch babies. Babies begin to reproduce the language they hear. Even though babies can't form words yet, they can try out the way words sound to them.

Therefore, in order to talk, the baby must hear people talking, not only to become acquainted with the patterns of human speech, but to hear the actual sounds of the letters that form the words. Talking, singing parents are the baby's first and most important teachers; they are laying the essential foundations for future reading.

## TO NAME IS TO KNOW

Questions are not only signs of a child's growing grasp of language, but of the child's growing mind, of a striving for knowledge, of an understanding of this incredibly complex world. Not to answer questions is to cut off inquiry, the principal means by which humankind has climbed out of ignorance into knowledge.

Babies may delight in knowing and naming the small world around them. Even before an infant attempts to speak, he or she listens to the caring adult using words, identifying objects, naming names; and slowly baby responds.

First, his whole body responds. When mother holds up a bottle and says, "Milk," baby's arms jump, his legs pump, his head moves eagerly. Baby's whole being identifies the object and the sound of its name as the answer to his stomach's crying need.

Then, in the fullness of time, baby responds to just the *name* of the beloved object—if mother has habitually identified it for baby.

"Milk?" she asks. "My honey wants his milk now, doesn't he?" And "my honey" wiggles in delighted agreement.

And finally comes the day when baby can state his needs in words. "Mi-wuh!" baby shouts. "Mi-wuh! Mi-wuh!" (or sounds to that effect).

Mother shouts too!

"Milk!" she screams. "Baby said 'Milk,' everybody!"

Mother rushes to supply the request to a round of applause for baby's great accomplishment. He has not only recognized the power of words and their relation to reality, but he can use them for his own needs. He has at last crossed the threshold into human speech. He has laid the most important foundation for future reading.

# CHAPTER
# 3

# *The Walking, Talking Toddler*

## GIANT STEPS

When babies learn to take those first unsteady steps, they are passing into toddlerhood. Some babies toddle before they speak, others speak before walking, while still others seem to begin to practice both skills at once. And it doesn't matter a bit which way your baby accomplishes these momentous steps.

## THE RESPONSIVE TODDLER

Usually toddlers recognize and respond to words before they themselves can speak. They can respond to simple directions—if they feel like it. When asked to pick up their coats, or a favorite toy, toddlers are usually quick to do so, delighting in their increasing comprehension of language. Even in the more negative developmental stages (around two and a half and three and a half) when they refuse to comply with such requests, they are still showing that they understand the words. Furthermore, when adults describe the toddler's actions, they are reinforcing the youngster's vocabulary, as in the following:

Mrs. Barnes asks her fourteen-month-old daughter, Mary, "Where's the dog, Mary? Where's Mary's dog?"

Triumphantly, Mary staggers over to scoop up her favorite stuffed animal as Mrs. Barnes says, "Yes, that's Mary's dog. Mary picks up her dog and hugs him!"

Mr. Simon, when trying to feed his thirteen-month-old son, Justin, says, "Hey, Justin, you are grabbing the spoon! Do you want to feed yourself? Do you want the spoon? Okay, here's your spoon."

Justin grabs the spoon and starts to shovel the applesauce out of the plate as his father continues, "Atta boy, Justin, eat your applesauce. Put the spoon into your mouth, Justin. Hey, put that applesauce in your mouth, not on the floor!"

As all parents know, each child develops in a different way, at a different speed. Yet even the best of parents sometimes forget this important fact—especially when other parents begin to boast.

Linda Carney became upset when a friend remarked, "You should hear how much our boy Adam says! He's only eighteen months old, but he talks a blue streak. Of course, we don't understand a lot of it, but boy! can he rattle on! He's always on the go, too. My wife and I are pooped trying to keep up with him."

Linda says, "I have to admit that my first reaction was jealousy; my darling Barry, the same age as Adam, was still staggering around from chair to chair. And Barry still babbled merrily, with only a few real words. Next, I felt worried. Was something wrong with Barry? Was he developing normally?

"Then I caught myself. How dumb could I get? Of course Barry was okay! He was just different from Adam. He wasn't in a walking-talking race. He knows what I say to him, he can feed himself, and show me what he wants. And he isn't in any hurry, so why am I?"

Linda was right. Barry was a bright, responsive boy, developing in his own way at his own pace, as all children do. The only concern Linda might have had would be if Barry didn't seem to hear her, to understand any words yet. Then it would have been a good idea for Linda to check out the child's hearing ability with her doctor.

## FIRST WORDS

As the baby-toddler progresses from babbling and cooing, we begin to hear words that are best understood by loving parents.

> Young Julie's first nouns were "li" (for light), "Ma" (mother), "mahma" (for her security blanket). She also threw in a few verbal demands, such as "wah" (go for a walk), "baba" (take a bath), and "uh, uh" (pick me up).

Julie's scant vocabulary seemed much richer because of her body language. Pointing to desired objects, tugging at grownups' clothes, yelling, throwing, stamping—all added to her effectiveness. At fifteen months, she seemed well able to get what she wanted with a few words, though she surely was far advanced from just crying.

## HELPING LANGUAGE DEVELOP

When toddlers have broken the language code, how best can adults help them? By more of the same:
 · more talking
 · more naming people, places, objects
 · more explaining actions
 · more telling what will happen or what has happened in the daily rounds
 · continued reading.
Already Julie drags her favorite books daily to the adult of her choice, demanding:

"Weed, weed!" (read) "You want me to read you a story?"
the adult responds, making a full sentence from Julie's one
word. Also, the adult does not repeat Julie's difficulty in saying the letter *r*—cute as she sounds, she won't be helped by
hearing her baby word repeated. "Okay, come sit with me.
We'll read the story together."

As they sit close together, enjoying the warmth of the shared
experience, something very important is happening. Julie is
learning that those little black squiggles on the paper represent words—words that people speak. And she is learning to
deal with the abstract: these squiggles not only represent
words, but words strung together to make pictures in her
mind. Julie is developing her creative imagination, a process
that as far as we know, separates us from all other life forms.

With a serious and intent expression as she leans against her
adult, who knows what Julie is imagining as she listens? Does
she visualize a scene from everyday life or from a wildly
wonderful fantasyland? All we do know is that she is making
connections—connections between written squiggles and
spoken words, between print and speech, between words
and reality, between the mind of the writer and her own
interpretations.

Caroline Pratt, a great educator, once said, "Thinking is
the process of making connections." And reading to our
smallest children is one sure way to encourage and strengthen
that process.

## ENCOURAGING THE TODDLER'S SPEECH

So, we have been "reading" to our babies since they could sit
up. Many babies can turn pages and point to pictures of
objects they recognize by the age of fifteen months. We have
been looking at magazine pictures together, at the simple
cloth books that show domestic animals or objects in the
baby's world.

And we have been reciting to the baby: nursery jingles

("Rain, rain, go away, little Stevie wants to play"); activity jingles ("This little piggy went to market"); accounts of baby's day ("Jimmy is climbing the stairs—up one step, up two steps, up three steps . . ."). We've been singing to baby, also. No matter that our voice is cracked, that we can't carry a tune; we've been belting out hit tunes, old favorites, music made up for the moment ("Here we go, here we go, here we go to the store, early Monday morning!"). As Dr. Joseph Church, another well-known psychologist, tells us, we encourage babies to speak by speaking to them. Dr. Church goes on to say that we can "bathe" the baby in speech as we tend him—anything from telling him how much we love him to discussing the stock market reports, asking his political opinions, reciting poetry, singing the latest advertising jingle, or even roaring out "Old Man River."

## WHEN TODDLERS TALK BACK

We don't stop all these speech activities when babies become toddlers who begin to respond to us vocally. Now we have the equally important task of speaking to their interests in the language we want the toddler to learn. Instead of asking her opinion on the stock market, we may now want to ask questions that expect an answer. For instance, Linda Carney might ask Barry:

Barry, do you want to wear your red sweater, this sweater? Or do you want to wear your yellow sweater, this one?

Barry may grab one sweater, or he may not. But Linda has indicated that Barry is not just being talked to now, he is a partner in the dialogue. And he is being given an opportunity to make a choice—a basic step toward independence—in a limited way. If Barry doesn't choose, Linda goes on:

Yes, I think Barry wants to wear his yellow sweater. Lift your arms up, Barry—way, way up, so Mommy can put on your sweater. Good boy!

Of course, Linda will still sing to Barry at times, explain their activities and the names of objects to him, and read to him as she has always done. Barry may show his interest only by body language at first, by looking alert, smiling, clapping, or other positive reactions; but sooner or later comes the time when he and other toddlers who have been "well bathed" in speech will attempt more elaborate speech themselves.

As a baby begins to talk back, his language is very concrete. He uses few or no adjectives, adverbs, and other modifiers. One word stands for a whole sentence: 'Pawa" might mean "I want to go to the park." (And just to make sure the ignorant adult understands him, he may bring along his coat or cap!) Once the child can communicate in words, he or she has almost magical power over reality. The speaking child can create a new world with words.

However, we are warned that adult rebuffs, indifference, or hostility can wither up the child's desire to develop language. Though mentioned before, this warning bears repeating; if a baby's first words, his verbal attempts to communicate are ignored, the baby won't be encouraged to try more. And if the baby's mispronunciations are always corrected sharply, or people laugh at them, he may stop speaking. How would we feel if our first faltering attempts to speak French or Spanish were ridiculed? Or constantly corrected?

Of course, most babies eventually do speak, but in a more stilted way than the baby who freely experimented with language. The speech-neglected toddler may use words only for his or her own needs or wishes, not as a sympathetic response to others' speech.

Communication is a two-way process: those children deprived of this tool probably won't develop to their fullest potential, and may experience difficulty in learning to read.

———

## SELF TALK

Toddlers not only like to try communicating to others in words, they also love to talk to themselves. When alone, they babble and play with words and sounds. Parents often hear them talking away in their cribs. One parent kept notes on the variety of sounds made by her young son when he was alone. In the beginning he just tried out sounds (ah-oooh-oooh-gah). As time passed, he tried out variations on words and syllables (eaty, meaty, geety; mat, matty, jat, gat). Other children will sit poring over their picture books, making languagelike sounds. This playing with words is evidently an important step in firming up knowledge of language for learning babies. They need lots of practice, and talking to themselves and to others is the way they get it.

## ACTIVITIES FOR EXPANDING SPEECH

Luckily, helping children to enlarge their vocabularies, to grasp grammar and sentence structure, to speak our language, to encourage their comprehension of the spoken word, is not a difficult task. We do it in part by expanding what we've been doing since the baby was born: talking to and with them; singing to and with them; naming and explaining to them.

From the toddler stage onward, we need to support and encourage additional skills and activities:
- encourage their physical skills
- encourage them to explore and play independently
- enlarge their first-hand experiences
- give them materials for creative expression
- play games with them
- read to them.

## PHYSICAL SKILLS RELATED TO READING

Encouraging motor skills and providing materials for creative expression are usually all important for children's physical and play activities, but just as important, these activities also strengthen reading readiness. How? By developing large and small muscles; by developing eye and hand coordination; and by helping to develop an amazing process called "lateral dominance."

### Lateral Dominance

Lateral dominance means establishing either right- or left-handedness as the child grows. The left side of the brain controls the right-hand activities, just as the right side of the brain controls the left-hand, and this "crossover" takes time to become effective. This "dominance" affects the child's ability to recognize and write letters correctly. Thus, youngsters often reverse letters, such as writing *d* for *b*, before the transfer is completed, or may make those strange letters, called "mirror writing," that look correct in the mirror. These are other solid reasons to delay formal teaching until the child is physically ready, with either right- or left-handedness firmly established.

*Important Note*: Experts warn against trying to alter lateral dominance—for instance, trying to get a child to use the right hand instead of the left. Well-meant interference not only confuses the child, it doesn't work; and, worst of all, it may hurt the whole process. Instead, give children plenty of opportunity to use their hands—with materials like big crayons, clay, sand shovels, or puzzles—and let nature direct the result.

### Large Muscle Development

Large muscles need to be developed for a child to achieve better balance and coordination. The toddler needs to handle large objects, such as hollow blocks, soft block cubes, large stuffed toys; to climb, to walk, to run; to creep and crawl; to pull and to push with pull toys, toy cars, and other wheeled objects.

*Small Muscle Development*

For developing those small muscles that are needed for handling a pencil or scissors, youngsters need to try out crayons, play with clay (or mud!), use fingerpaints, work with cut-out toys and puzzles, bang on those small hammer toys, fit jigsaws or manipulate stacking toys, and, of course, have books to hold with pages to turn and pictures to look at.

At first glance, these activities don't seem to relate much to reading. But a second look may help us see the relationships better. For instance, to fit a jigsaw piece in place correctly, we have to match shapes, see the fine distinctions between one piece and another. This is one of the skills needed to tell the difference between a *b* or a *d*, or tell an *off* from an *of*. Fitting cut-out toys (cubes into cube-shaped holes, or triangles into their proper places) also strengthens this skill. Banging the right rod with the hammer, squishing and spreading fingerpaints, stacking nesting toys—all help develop the finger muscles (as well as give the toddlers lots of esthetic and physical fun). Good hand control is essential for forming letters later on.

Of course, handling books is obviously related to reading skills: even the youngest toddler learns to turn a book around to see the pictures correctly. Soon toddlers catch on to the fact that the book, with its peculiar black squiggles, represents a story that the child loves to hear. And love of hearing the story is a great incentive for reading.

## ENCOURAGING EXPLORATION AND PLAY

When babies become toddlers, a whole new world of exploration opens up for them. They are still predominantly using all their senses: touching, looking, tasting, smelling, listening. But it is this driving urge to explore and to know that will develop, if encouraged, into the same drive to explore and cope with reading later on. Parents have a bigger problem now: how to keep toddlers safe, yet allow them to satisfy the great urge to explore? How to help them to develop those skills that will be so important later on in school?

> Johnny is driving me crazy! He's always on the go; if I turn him loose, he's into everything! Pulls things off the shelves, off the coffee table. When I stick him in his playpen or in his room, he begins to yell . . . of course, *after* he's messed up everything there, too. By now, if he isn't yelling, I'm scared he's up to something dangerous. So I keep running to look. I don't have time to myself anymore.

Sound familiar? Most of us have had moments when we feel like this. When we yearn for "the good old days" when Johnny was safely a non-walker or a non-creeper.

Such occasional feelings are natural—if fleeting. (We *really* don't want to keep Johnny a baby.) We want Johnny to have what he needs for his best development. At the same time, we don't want him to get hurt—and we don't want to knock ourselves out taking care of him, either. So what do we do? Let's ask ourselves some questions:

- Do toddlers need freedom to explore at home?
- If so, can we safely provide it?
- Does this freedom tie in with preparing a child for reading?

Yes, yes, and yes! But take heart—there are ways to answer these questions and keep Johnny's exploring drive alive without being "driven crazy."

*Exploring at Home*

Free play activity at home is the toddler's first experience of the larger world. Toddlers love to "toddle" from couch to chair, from table to shelf, grabbing and pulling as they go. You can imagine the shambles a free-roving toddler can create. Not to mention the possible damage to himself.

Some people think the only answer to both problems (damage to the child and to the house) is to limit the child's movements, either in a playpen or in the baby's room. This may work for a while, but not continually. Remember how Johnny's mother had to keep running to check on him? And how frustrated Johnny became? How cramped in limited space, how bored with the same toys? What we may not realize is that too many limitations may stifle that urge to discover that is so vital to his future learning.

So what's the answer? How can we give our Johnnies or Jennies house-freedom yet keep them safe and ourselves sane? By toddler-proofing the home!

Toddler-proofing the home means:

- removing treasured objects from the toddler's reach
- removing all dangerous objects from the toddler's reach
- removing sharp-edged furniture, slippery rugs, glass of all kinds
- locking medicine chests, cupboards containing poisonous materials, such as most cleaners and polishes (or placing these objects out of toddler's reach)
- covering unused electrical outlets.

Then squat down and view your place from a toddler's eye level. You will often discover and can remove other objects that could be harmful yet fascinating to a young child. Remember, the changes are not forever: toddlers keep on growing in wisdom as well as in strength, and what was removed can soon be replaced.

Toddler-proofing can make parents feel a lot freer to go about their business without having constantly to "check on Johnny" locked away in his room. They'll be freer to keep an eye on their toddler's doings, and to watch reactions more naturally. Children are only this age once: it's a great experience to see them investigate their home world without getting jittery about it.

I don't think any of us would want to copy one woman I met. We sat in her living room having tea, while her toddler staggered about. But every time he touched anything on the coffee table, she slapped his hand! Shocked, I asked, "Why don't you just put those fascinating objects away for the time being?"

She replied, "Henry has to learn *not* to touch things! I believe in beginning right now to teach him the right way."

Poor Henry! And poor mother. What Henry had learned was the "wrong way." He would scrunch up his face, eyes closed, and suffer the slaps; then he would go right after the next thing he wanted! What he must have learned is that if you take something, you'll be punished—but go ahead and take it anyhow. Henry, like most toddlers, wasn't ready to understand his mother's reasoning. He didn't think about what might happen in the future (getting slapped) but did what he wanted in the present (grabbing things). Actually, Henry came off better than some children. This kind of reaction could have caused Henry to stop exploring, to curb his natural curiosity, and cut off some basic learning processes.

*Objects to Explore*
Now that you've toddler-proofed, what's left to satisfy the toddler's need to explore? New objects can be placed on a low shelf or in a box where the toddler can reach them, such as:

- old magazines, a few sturdy books, interesting pictures: these start the young child forming a relationship to books that will not only lead to successful reading later but, hopefully, will become a lifelong satisfaction
- a few toys, blocks, stuffed dolls
- some "found materials" (pieces of material, wheels, straws, sponges, discarded objects that open, close, snap, or zip)
- some favorite, safe household objects (small broom, dustpan, pots, pans)

Don't overwhelm the child with all these things at one time. Try changing them when the toddler no longer seems interested. Make sure that there is always a book or two to look at—and keep reading to your child each day.

*The Exploring Mind*
Not only can the home provide for the child's muscle devel-

opment, it can also help answer another urgent need of the child: the need to know, the need to develop his mind, the same mind that will explore reading later on. This innate curiosity, if stimulated, will lead the child later to accept the intellectual demands of school, such as math, science, history, and, of course, reading, upon which all the other subjects depend. However, if the child's present urge to explore and experiment is discouraged, it will be hard, if not impossible, to reawaken it later. Opportunities to explore, to test things out, to question, to compare, to understand, to know, are essential. As one father relates:

> I love to watch Lynn thinking—I can see her making conclusions so often. For instance, she spent a long time fitting pans together. She tried vainly to get a big pan into a little pan; then I saw the look of deep satisfaction when she put a little pan in a big pan. She fitted all the pans this way. Then she brought them to me and proudly said, "All go in."
>
> That little kid's testing things all the time, making comparisons, drawing conclusions. And that's what learning's all about—not just memorizing, but understanding. She won't just be a reader; she'll dig out the meaning of the words!

I myself watched a two-year-old poring over a cardboard book filled with pictures of animals she knew. She turned the pages over again and again, talking to herself:

> Little dog, big dog. Little kitty, big kitty. Dog eat, dog not eat. Ball. Kitty ball, dog ball.

She wasn't interested in a plot or a story. She was making her own observations and comparisons; she was learning and thinking independently. She was laying a basic foundation for future reading.

Another father told me:

> Kenny has always loved to turn the light switch off and on. The other day he asked, "Where light go?" I was stumped. I

can't even explain electricity to myself! Luckily, he answered, "Light go to sleep." I realized Kenny is making connections based on his own experiences. Sure, they may not be the right conclusions, but they're okay for him at this stage. I have to keep remembering so I don't overload him with information. The important thing is that Kenny is thinking, putting two and two together—even if he ends up with five!

Sure, I give him right answers, too, when they would mean something. Like, when he asked where the water came from, I showed him the water pipes. But when he asked me where a very small beetle lived (he found it on the carpet), I had to say I didn't know. I think it's good for kids to know that grownups don't know everything, that they can learn, too.

Right now, Kenny's learning from first-hand experiences. Later on, he'll be learning more from what he reads and has read to him. But because he's had time to learn this way, first-hand, he'll be able to get a lot from secondhand experiences, like reading. He's got a solid foundation to build on.

Toddlers are always stretching their minds with the knowledge they discover in the environment. They are observing, measuring, comparing, making connections and drawing conclusions—these are comprehension skills, the same skills they need to differentiate words, to understand what they mean. When the environment is rich in objects that attract toddlers and when they can explore freely, they learn more. Reading without making connections is a meaningless process. The child whose environment is restricted and barren will not only have less knowledge but will be less developed in the skill of creative thinking, and certainly less ready to take that tremendous step into the reading process.

## PLAYING GAMES WITH TODDLERS

Toddlers want to interact with their caregivers. Increasingly, they attempt to communicate with their beloved adults, both in speech and in action. They are making the first attempts to break out of an all "me" world to the bigger concepts of a "me-you" world, often in a playful way.

> Fourteen-month-old Lisa pulled off the fireman's hat she was wearing and tried to put it on her mother's head. Her understanding mother obligingly ducked her head so Lisa could do so. Then, smiling delightedly, Lisa pulled the hat off, stuck it on her own head, then tried to replace it on her mother again. Mother attempted to change the pattern by placing the firehat on Lisa's teddy bear. Lisa smiled, but snatched the hat off to replace it on Mother's head again.

This is play on a toddler's level. The main ingredient is repetition—which may seem monotonous to an adult. But the youngster is not only strengthening a relationship but testing out skills and concepts: the hat won't fit if placed upside down; the adult and child both wear hats on their heads; the child can put hats on adults as well as vice-versa. Simplistic concepts to us, maybe, but news to the toddler. And perhaps the most important result is the growth of a trusting relationship with adults—a very necessary ingredient for healthy growth and basic to future reading development.

Verses and stories for the very young that are full of repetitions and refrains delight this age child. *Mother Goose Rhymes, The Little Red Hen, The Gingerbread Boy* are good examples of rhythm and refrain. But best of all are your own made-up stories about your child's day. Fill them with repetition and direct action. Your child will respond not only with delight but often with physical accompaniment. As Bill Kinney chanted, "Johnny went up one step, hop, hop, hop, Johnny went up two steps, hop, hop, hop, Johnny went up three steps, hop, hop, hop," his son began jumping around the room, grinning broadly and joining in, "'op 'op 'op!"

## STRENGTHENING PRE-READING BOOK EXPERIENCES

The best way of preparing toddlers for reading (and other school experiences) is twofold:

- · first, by allowing them to develop *all* their potential in a safe and loving environment
- · and second, by creating a "world of words" for them, both in print and in spoken language.

The first preparation has already been discussed; let's look now at how we can best create that "world of words."

## TELLING TODDLERS STORIES

By the time a child is two, a regular daily story time should be established. Most parents and other caregivers find that story time fits naturally into going-to-bed time. It provides a restful transition from the world of activity to the world of sleep. Perhaps it also stimulates sweet dreams. An editor recalls:

> The best moment of each day was Dad's story at bedtime. When I was tucked in, he'd sit in the dark on the bed, weaving his tales of magical rabbits and other beasts, spun from his imagination. One by one the other children, considered too old for baby stories, would creep in to listen. I don't remember the stories, but I sure remember the warm, cozy, *loved* feeling they gave me.

Telling stories to children is the most direct way to reach them. Not everyone can create "magical rabbits," but anyone can relate the doings of the real child. Even babies respond to a personalized story.

### Recalling the Child's Day

Toddlers listen eagerly to any accounting of their doings from a simple recall of a routine activity to the savoring of a special event. Here are some examples:

### "Linda's Day"

Linda hopped out of bed this morning.
She put on her pink pants
and her yellow sunsuit
with the three green ducks.
She put on her white socks—
all by herself.
She put on her red sneakers—
all by herself.
And Mommy tied the laces.
Then Linda went hop, hop, hop
off to the playground.
She played all morning
with Marty, and Peter, and Lara,
and Amy—don't forget Amy!
Then, hoppity-hop,
Linda came home again.
She took off her yellow sunsuit.
Linda had lunch.
And then a good nap.
Then Linda played—
all by herself
with magazines, and pots, and pans
while Mommy fixed dinner.
Then Linda had a bath.
She put on her bunny pajamas
and hopped into bed.
Now, Linda closes one eye,
now the other eye.
Stay closed, Eyes!
The Baby Bear is right beside Linda,
and the moon shines into her room.
Goodnight, Baby Bear.
Goodnight, Big Moon.
Goodnight, goodnight, Linda Darling.

### "Peter's Trip"

Peter went to the city today, didn't he?
Yes, he went with Grandpa and me.

Remember how fast the train went?
Right by all the houses
and trees and roads and people.
Then right over the big rackety bridge
and into the dark tunnel.
Then the train stopped.
Peter and Grandpa and I walked and walked
through the station,
down the street, down another street.
We went in a very tall building—
a skyscraper!
We rode way up in an elevator
to Grandpa's office.
Peter typed on the typewriter.
Then we all ate spaghetti
in Grandpa's favorite restaurant.
And we all came home
in the long clickity-clack train!

### Using Fantasy

Young children respond to light fantasies about their daily deeds, too. By creatively enlarging on their everyday experiences, parents encourage the child's own imagination.

Some parents may feel ill at ease with this approach. One of them, Elva Harris, asks, "Doesn't such exaggeration encourage children to lie? I think my children should tell what's real, not make things up."

Of course, we would agree with Elva Harris: we *do* want our young ones to distinguish between fact and fantasy. But such distinction is often hard for young toddlers who are still learning what is real, what is unreal. Toddlers don't really lie; at this stage, they do mix fact and fantasy.

That's why we encourage toddlers' exploration of the world: so that they can find out what is real. We also believe that gentle fantasy stories offer opportunities to express feelings and emotions which are equally important. For example, the following small fantasy centers on jealousy and lonesomeness.

### "Tony Has No Wagon"

Marika had a brand-new red wagon, with a silver bell. Tony didn't have a brand-new wagon with a silver bell. Tony felt angry. "I'm not going to stay around here," he said. "I'll fly away to the moon." So Tony flew away to the moon. It was cold and lonesome there, and Tony's spacesuit itched. "So I'll live by myself on the beach," he said. But the wind blew and sand got in his eyes at the beach. And there wasn't anyone to play with. "I'll let you play with my wagon if you come home," said Marika. So Tony came home and he and Marika played with the new wagon all morning. And that's the end!

In hearing this fantasy, Tony knew it was a "pretend" story about real happenings. But it expressed Tony's emotions and feelings in a way that more matter-of-fact accounts couldn't do. Some of the lasting values of fantasy are that they present truths in a non-preachy way and, being one step removed from the real event, allow us to look at the deeper meanings of our experiences. This is true for children as well as for adults.

*Introducing Humor*

Fantasy about daily events also gives us a chance for humor. Most humor for very young children is based on incongruity—the right thing in the wrong place. One reason why small fry seldom laugh at funny stories is that they haven't acquired enough knowledge to recognize incongruities. We must start with the very familiar in an absurd setting to expose the youngest to the relaxing joys of humor.

### "The Mixed-Up Billy Goat"

One day Billy Goat saw Brenda's wash hanging on the line.
"Why shouldn't I wear Brenda's clothes?" Billy asked.
No one answered.
So Billy Goat took down Brenda's red socks and put them on his ears.
Next, he took down Brenda's blue cap and put it on his tail.
Last of all, he took down Brenda's blue jeans and tied them around his neck!

"Look at me! Look at me! I'm all dressed up!" Billy Goat yelled.
Brenda came out.
She said, "Those are my clothes,
not your clothes, Billy Goat.
You have them on wrong.
I'll show you how to put them on right."
Brenda took her red socks off Billy's Goat's ears.
Then she put them on herself.
Where did she put them?
Yes, on her feet.
Next, she took her blue cap
off Billy Goat's tail
and put it on herself.
Where did she put it?
Yes, she put it on her head!
(The story could go on to the rest of Brenda's dressing.)

Simpler forms of this kind of fun could be as short as:

> Where do Brenda's socks go?
> On her nose? (No.)
> On her ears? (No!)
> On her feet? (Yes!)

Both stories show incongruities clearly, and help toddlers understand their humorous aspects. But both stories also help the child understand the name and use of his clothes and his body parts—details that kindergarten children are expected to know.

### What to Avoid

However, there are some areas to be avoided at the toddler level. First, the fantasy shouldn't be frightening. The toddler, still struggling to know the real from the unreal, isn't sure that witches, Dracula, or ghosts aren't real. But the same toddler is fairly sure that teddy bears don't eat lollypops, that rabbits don't dress in snowsuits, that cats and dogs don't cook or bake in the kitchen. So any tale around such activities is acceptable fantasy.

Small children don't relate to love stories, have little ability to cope with death and other violent disasters. The best fantasies for toddlers deal with events they can comprehend within the limits of their own small experiences.

## READING TODDLERS STORIES

Sticking to the realm of a toddler's experience is a good rule of thumb for choosing books. Let's look at a very familiar folk tale. *The Little Red Hen* has always appealed to the very young. Why? First of all, the hen's activities can be comprehended by toddlers. Even though they include some unknown activities, such as "carrying grain to the mill," their meaning can be guessed from the preceding events and from the pictures. Children readily identify with the Little Red Hen: they, too, are small and no doubt feel that their activities may seem unimportant to other family members. Youngsters feel a triumphant vindication when Hen gets to eat the bread "all by herself!" This strongly appeals to their developing sense of fairness.

The second reason for *The Little Red Hen*'s durability is the style of writing. Young children respond to rhythms and refrains, both of which abound in this story. The rhythmic lines—"Who will help me plant the wheat?" "Who will help me water the wheat?" "Who will help me cut the wheat?"—satisfy a youngster's desire for orderly predictability. The refrains are not only catchy, but tempt children to repeat them, thus drawing them into "reading" the story with the adult—a fine way to prepare for real reading later on.

> "Not me," said the Cat.
> "Not me," said the Dog.
> "And not me," said the Pig.

After hearing this refrain several times to the Little Red Hen's questions, what child wouldn't want to join in?

The text is memorable, too, for its simplicity and quick

pace. We aren't told anything about the setting or the characters. We don't know where they live, or how. All such matters are irrelevant to the story line. Every sentence carries the plot forward, with no stops for scenery descriptions or explanations. No judgment is made about the behavior of the Hen's friends: the listeners are considered smart enough to make judgments themselves. And the ending vindicates the listeners' need to have the Little Red Hen win out.

## CHOOSING STORIES FOR TODDLERS

At this point, you may well be thinking, "So many points to be made from a simple story like *The Little Red Hen*?"

Yes, for these are the basic points to consider in choosing any story for toddlers:

*Suitability of Plot*: Do the ideas and actions in the story seem right for young children?

*Message of Story*: Do you agree with it? Is it right for young children? Will they understand it?

*Suitability of Writing*: Is the story written simply enough? Does it have rhythms and refrains? Is it fun to read aloud?

*Sturdiness of Book*: Are the pages firmly sewn together? Can a child hold and turn the pages easily? Is the cover strong and fastened well to the book?

*Attractiveness of the Art*: Toddlers don't have enough experience yet to deal with abstract ideas or objects. Are the pictures clear enough to be readily identified? Are they done carefully, with good details? Do they match the text? Do *you* like them?

If you say yes to these questions, you probably have a good story for toddlers and preschool children. Choose the very simplest story for the toddler; save the more plotted story for the older threes and the four-year-olds.

Let's look at some appropriate books for the eighteen- to twenty-four-month-old child. Remember, these ages are only approximate; some children will respond to the books earlier, while others may want to stick with their "baby books" longer—or just listen to "told stories."

*Where to Find Them*
This land of abundance provides many books for young children; most of them are to be found in libraries, book stores, and supermarkets. Unfortunately, the most available, those from supermarkets, are usually the least distinguished; low cost, not excellence of text and art, is often the prime consideration. But even here, a careful search will find some good choices, such as the Little Golden Books or the Random House paperbacks. As always, look first for what appeals to your particular child. The subjects that are most appealing to toddlers are:
- animals
- things that move or go
- daily special events in their lives
- all kinds of people interacting with children
- objects in their environment.

## A SAMPLING OF GOOD BOOKS FOR TODDLERS

*Board Books*
In general, board books have heavy cardboard covers and contain relatively few pages. They usually show a few familiar objects, animals, or scenes from the young child's world.

> *I Can Do It Myself*, June Goldsborough (Golden)
> While the actions pictured may be those of a slightly older child, toddlers will recognize them as their next stepping stones.
> *Farm Animals*, Nancy Sears (Random House)
> Large, clear pictures of domestic animals.
> *Baby Animals*, Gerry Swart (Golden)
> Large colored pictures for the child who has seen these animals in the zoo.

*My Yard*, Heinz Kluetmeier (Golden)
> These clear colored photographs of children swinging, running, playing in a sandbox, really illustrate a playground or park rather than a yard, so the book appeals to city toddlers also.

*The Touch-Me Book*, Pat and Eve Witte (Golden)
> Objects made of different materials (a sponge, fur, string, feather) not only can be looked at, but felt on each page. A sturdy book full of sensory experiences.

*Dr. Foster and Other Rhymes, A First Nursery Rhyme Book* (Crown)
> Lively double-spread pictures that flow across opposing pages are filled with homely details.

*This Is My House*, John E. Johnston (Golden)
> In this sturdy shape book, each page shows another room filled with familiar objects, each labeled.

### Poetry Books and Mother Goose Rhymes

Poetry appeals to all ages. Toddlers will delight in the following because of the strong rhythm and repetitive refrains.

*Mother Goose Rhymes*, Alice and Martin Provensen (Random House)
> Fine artists with an understanding of the realistic clarity young children need in book pictures.

*Mother Goose Nursery Rhymes*, Arthur Rackham (Viking)
> A master's masterly rendition, full of traditional details.

*The Tall Book of Mother Goose*, Feodor Rojankovsky (Harper)
> Finely painted, natural-looking groups of children.

(You may find other wonderfully pictured Mother Gooses on your own.)

*Nibble, Nibble*, Margaret Wise Brown (Addison Wesley)
> Delicate writing full of sensory feeling may appeal to the youngest.

*Bam! Zoom! Bam! A Building Book*, Eve Merriam
(Walker)
  Lots of noisy sounds and swinging rhythms.
*Rockabye, Baby*, Eloise Wilkins (Random House)
  Nursery songs and cradle games; small verses for sim-
  ple finger games to play with your favorite toddler. A
  "shape" book.

## Object Books

"Object," or naming, books dominate the early years. They
provide countless opportunities for children to identify, classify, and sort out people, places, animals, and objects in their
world. They foster a great deal of language experience that is
so necessary to reading readiness.

*Little Word Book* and *My House*, Richard Scarry
(Golden/Western)
  Though meant for older children, the pictures are en-
  joyed by toddlers, too.
*I Spy: Picture Book of Objects in a Child's World* and *I
Hear: Sounds in a Child's World*, Lucille Ogle and Tina
Thoburn (American Heritage)
  Popular favorites, both books are full of small, clear
  pictures of everyday objects; great for "naming."
*Big Book of Real Trucks* and *Big Book of Real Fire Engines*,
George Zaffo (Grosset and Dunlap)
  Very little text, but big, gorgeous pictures for young-
  sters interested in busy streets.
*Cars and Trucks and Things That Go*, Richard Scarry
(Golden/Western)
  A whole panorama of various vehicles driven by Scar-
  ry's charming little animals.
*Busy Houses*, Richard Scarry (Golden/Western)
  A board book showing many household chores en-
  acted by busy animals.
*A Child's Book of Everyday Things*, Thomas Matthiesen
(Platt & Munk)

Handsome, bright pictures of objects indoors and outdoors.

*A Good Day, A Good Night*, Cindy Wheeler (Lippincott)
A cat sees day and night objects; simple, satisfying.

*The Rabbit; The Snow; The Blanket; The Dog*, all by John Burningham (Crowell)
Fine illustrations, simply done, all within the scope of a young child's experience.

*Animal Books*

*Kittens Are Like That*, Jan Pfloog (Golden/Western)

*I Am a Kitten* and *I Am a Puppy*, Risom and Pfloog (Golden/Western)
Pfloog's clear depictions of baby animals are loved by youngsters.

*I Am a Bunny*, Richard Scarry (Golden/Western)
A charming bunny just the right size to hold.

*Animal Babies*, Henry McNaught (Random House)
Clear photos (by Ylla) of real animal babies.

*Will That Wake Mother?* Martha McKeen Welch (Dodd Mead)
Charming, clear photos of three kittens with the simplest of plots and a satisfying ending guaranteed to please youngsters.

*Puppies Need Someone to Love*, Hinds and Goldsborough (Golden)
A Golden Look-Look Book, this small paperback is full of lovable dogs.

*Pat the Bunny*, Dorothy Kunhardt (Golden/Western)
A classic tactile book that offers toddlers the chance to experience the feel of many textures. Has many imitators.

*Animals in the Woods*, Michele Chopin Roosevelt (Random House)
Charming, realistic pictures of small creatures.

*My Day on the Farm*, Chiyoko Nakatani (Crowell)
Simple pictures of cows, pigs, sheep, and goats that

will give small children a beginning concept of what farm animals do.

*The Little Kitten*, Judy and Phoebe Dunn (Random House)
> One of a winning series of wonderful photos of familiar animals with children.

*People Books*

The most important features in young children's environments are the people around them; toddlers are especially attracted to other children. Books that clearly show humans in action, whether in photos or in pictures, are sure winners with the youngest family members.

*Babies*, Gyo Fujikawa (Grosset & Dunlap)
> Sweet, rather saccharine art, but full of all kinds of human babies.

*Playing; Dressing; Friends; Family; Working*, all by Helen Oxenbury (Wanderer Books, Simon & Schuster)
> These books contain delicately drawn, clearly colored pictures that show people and everyday objects.

*Tommy Takes a Bath* (Houghton Mifflin) and *Betsy's Baby Brother* (Random House), both by Gunilla Wolde
> Two children engage in everyday activities that youngsters will relate to and delight in through repeated "readings."

*Bodies* and *Faces*, Barbara Brenner and George Ancona (Dutton)
> Wonderful, joyous photographs of all kinds of people, young and old, with all kinds of faces and shapes.

*Around and Around—Love*, Betty Miles (Knopf)
> Another happy festival of people showing all kinds of love. Toddlers respond wholeheartedly to these fine photographs of real people.

*How Do I Put It On? An I-Can-Do-It-All-by-Myself Book*, Shigeo Watanabe (Philomel)
> In this award-winning book, an article of clothing is

pictured on one page; on the opposing page, a droll bear is trying to put it on in the wrong way. A great book for initiating humor.

*Ben's ABC Day*, Terry Berger and Alice Kandell (Lothrop, Lee & Shepard)

Excellent photographs of a young child's typical activities. While cleverly alphabetized, the pictures will attract those younger than ABC learners, too.

*What Sadie Sang*, Eve Rice (Greenwillow)

Today Sadie wants to ride in her stroller, though she can walk. She sings one word all day long: "Ghee! Ghee!"

*You Go Away*, Dorothy Carey and Lois Axeman (A. Whitman)

Lots of pictures of children and people going away and coming back. Includes peek-a-boo and a child who cries as Mama leaves. Reassuring depiction of a traumatic experience.

*Look at Me*, Ryllis A. Lindlay and Beatrice Derwinski (Broadman)

Great pictures of a one-year-old creeping, climbing, washing, eating. Dated, but very identifiable. Hard to find but worth the search.

## Simple Plotted Storybooks

While stories made up and told about each child are still great favorites, older toddlers are ready for simple plots, such as in the following books:

*Davy's Day*, Lois Lenski (Walck)

A simply told account of one small boy's day.

*Three Kittens*, Mirra Ginsberg (Crown)

Beautiful pictures, sparse text.

*A Box with Red Wheels*, Maud and Miska Petersham (Macmillan)

Friendly farm animals discover a surprise.

*Goodnight, Moon*, Margaret Wise Brown (Harper)

This book is a *must* for young children. For some eighteen-month-old toddlers, it becomes the first and most beloved book. Other youngsters love it at two, three, four, five, or six years. But all children should have an opportunity to experience this story.

Why is it so successful? There are many different opinions, but the rhythmic, sleepy cadence of the text and the fascinating pictures of the slowly darkening room have produced a small masterpiece that youngsters want to hear over and over.

# CHAPTER
## 4

# *Twos and Young Threes*

## DEVELOPING UNDERSTANDING

Just as physical abilities have developed for children who have lived almost twice as long as toddlers, so have their understanding and knowledge broadened. Now most children can comprehend and learn from simple plotted stories; can grasp and learn from concept books; may begin to distinguish a letter and a number or two; can handle simple puzzle boards and games. They can begin to use materials in a more meaningful way. They can understand and follow more detailed directions such as, "Put your toy on the *bottom* shelf." Frequently now they are apt to follow through a planned or self-initiated activity.

### Longer Attention Span

At three-year-old Peter's birthday party he and a friend were making clay sausages. Two-and-a-half-year-old Marcy joined them. She then announced that she was going to make muffins. After Marcy patted her clay for a while, she went over to some low shelves containing a miscellaneous assortment of pans, pots, boats, animals, a purse or two, some spoons. First she carried a pot and a pan back to the clay table, and filled them both with clay. Then, dumping the clay out again, Marcy carried the utensils back to the shelf. This time she found a muffin pan and returned to the table. After putting some clay in a few muffin cups, Marcy got up and returned to the shelves. Chanting, "Muffins, muffins!" she dumped the contents of the shelves onto the floor. Then she returned to the table carrying a pot and a spoon. She emptied her clay into the pot and stirred it with the spoon, still chanting. Next, she carefully spooned the clay into the muffin pan, carried it over to Peter's toy stove, and stuck it in the oven. "Muffins cooking," she said with evident satisfaction.

Six months earlier, Marcy would not have carried through such an elaborate process. Her attention span now allows her to initiate and carry through a task to a logical conclusion.

### New Levels of Understanding

Marcy's play is a typical example of some of the major changes that develop as a child nears three years of age.

First of all, Marcy shows quite a detailed understanding of muffin-baking: she recalled the necessity of stirring the ingredients first, pouring the muffins into the muffin pan, then baking them in the oven. Even though she made a few false starts, she corrected them. Secondly, she carried through her intention of muffin-making—at her own pace and level of understanding. She was no longer content just to bang some clay into "muffins," but needed to reproduce more of the real process. At the same time, she ignored the mess she had created on the floor and didn't carry the play beyond the baking stage. But Marcy is exercising many of the skills that will prepare her for future reading: she shows a growing attention span, a knowledge of sequence, attention to details, and an ability to follow directions.

But it's also important to remember that while Marcy showed this kind of interest and comprehension at two and a half, her playmates may not. Some children will show such details in their play at an earlier age, others won't be interested until later. Children develop at different paces, at different times—and there isn't any "right" or "wrong" time, just different ones. However, in general, twos and young threes are interested in and able to grasp more details in a book or "told" story. In their play they show an understanding of more concepts, like *on* or *off*, *over* or *under*, *many* or *few*.

*A Word to the Wise:* Remember that these early years of development usually have a "see-saw" effect; children seem to go through periods of calm contentedness followed by more disruptive behavior. The best advice is to "possess our souls in patience" and wait out the periods of upset, avoiding arguments and confrontations as much as possible. As usual, individual children may not follow this pattern.

## FIRST-HAND EXPERIENCE STILL BASIC

Learning is still firmly based on first-hand experiences: children won't understand "red" unless they have seen red engines or worn red clothes. The child is not yet ready for formal teaching; even if he likes to recite the ABC's, he is still playing with this skill, and rattling off the alphabet may have no more real meaning for the young child than a string of nonsense words. The best teaching at this age is to give children wide experience in the real world and appropriate material to play out these experiences, and to read to them a wide variety of books. Children—like all of us—learn best what they teach themselves. Children will take from all experiences, in real life or in books, what they can understand. Our job is to give them the best suitable experiences, materials, and books we can find on their level of understanding. We can also play some simple games with them to help them sort out, classify, form new concepts, observe detail, and make conclusions—skills that will be very important later in school.

## SIMPLE GAMES

Adults have played games with children from babyhood on. At first, the games were as simple as "peek-a-boo" (hiding one's face behind fingers, then pulling them away to smile at baby) and "How big is baby? So-o-o-o-o big!" (stretching baby's arms up high).

With twos and young threes, the games develop naturally into skill-reinforcement play—a very academic-sounding phrase, but easy and fun to do! Games like "I Spy," "Hide the Ball," "Who Said That?" are good examples.

*I Spy*

This is equally good for naming objects, people, toys, or colors. For instance, the adult may say, "I spy with my little eye . . . a brown teddy bear!" (Or, "the yellow cat," "a red sled.") "Do you see it, too?" Or the adult may say, "I spy with my little eye . . . something red! Can you see it, too?" The youngster either names the object (snowsuit, apple, sock) or touches it.

For these very young children, start with only *one* object to be chosen. If your three-year-old seems to be very adept at "I Spy" you can try a bit more difficult version: "I spy *two* red things on the shelf. Can you see them?" This game helps children discern colors and objects more keenly and quickly—a very good preparation for reading readiness.

*Hide the Ball*

In its simplest version, the adult places a large object, like a ball, in some fairly obvious place—behind a chair, in a chair, on a shelf. "Can you find the ball?" asks the adult. Gleefully, the youngster discovers and grabs it.

From this simple beginning, the game can be extended to encourage dialogue with the child and some educated guesses. For instance, the adult places a big beach ball under a chair, then asks a series of questions. "Is the ball in Mommy's purse? Is it in Jimmy's pocket? Could it be under the toy truck?" Give Jimmy a chance to say "no" to all of the places that are far too small for the big beach ball to be hidden. Finally, ask, "Then where could it be?" and give Jimmy the pleasure of telling you that it's under the chair.

Children will want to play this over and over; some will want to hide the ball themselves. If they do, the adult should "ham it up" by pretending to search all over for the ball, though it is usually in plain sight.

This game helps the child develop the skills he needs in order to make discoveries—making guesses, testing them out, making judgments (a big ball can't fit in Mommy's purse), persevering until the job is accomplished.

### Who Said That?

This is a good game to play during those inevitable moments of waiting—waiting for a bus, waiting in the doctor's office, taking a long ride in a car. Such games not only help pass the time without too much fretting, but also help sharpen the child's listening skills. The adult might say, "Sh! I heard something! Something that said, 'Meow, meow.' Do you know who said that?"

As the child catches on to the game, you can give slightly harder clues, such as "I heard something that said, 'Vroom, vroom!' Who said that? Yes, a car said that."

Many children will want to have a turn telling you what they heard. At first, some of their statements may sound very silly. ("I heard something say, "Gribby-grabby!'") If the adult keeps the game attuned to real sounds, usually the children will use one or two real sounds, too. The important thing is to encourage the child to express himself; no matter how ridiculous he sounds, he is taking another giant step toward a satisfying exchange of ideas with adults. Even more important, the child is developing good listening skills that are basic to following directions and understanding explanations.

### What These Games Do

Of course, there are many other easy games for looking and listening, but don't forget the other senses. Try smelling: "I smell something sharp and oily. Yes, it's the gas going into the gas tank." Or feeling: "I just touched something small, soft, and furry. Yes, it's the hamster." You will probably think of others to intrigue your special child.

The importance of these little sensory games is threefold:

- First, they help a child use all her senses in a playful way.
- Second, while still using concrete objects, the child also has to use her mental powers. (Where could a big ball be hidden? What kind of animal makes that sound? What does "sharp and oily" smell like?)
- Third, the child is experiencing an adult/child, teacher/pupil relationship, which is a necessary basis for school learning. Children who have had such satisfactory communications with adults will be more trusting, more eager to accept a teacher's directions in school, and thus will be more open to and benefit more from formal teaching later on.

## USING SIMPLE PUZZLE BOARDS

Two-year-old and young three-year-old children usually enjoy simple puzzle boards. These are the puzzles that have whole shapes of recognizable objects that can be lifted out of the boards. For instance, on a puzzle board showing a lake and a beach, the following objects might be the removable parts: a boat, a child, a dog, a beach umbrella, a beach ball. The child should not only be able to fit these objects into their proper places, but to name them also. Frequently, a child can't name a familiar object such as a fire hydrant, a mailbox, or a stoplight. These puzzles offer a good opportunity for extending a youngster's vocabulary.

Some of the whole-object puzzles may create a problem. Many puzzle boards have tiny knobs attached to the puzzle pieces that the child is expected to lift out. Often these are too small for young fingers to grasp readily. The best method of detaching puzzle pieces is to turn the board upside down and dump out all the movable parts. Then the child can have the fun of fitting each puzzle piece back into the proper place without frustration.

When introducing puzzle boards to young children it is best to let them see the board with the dropout pieces in place. Then dump the pieces and ask the child to put them back where they belong. It's also a good idea to encourage the child to name the dropout pieces. And, when the child has had success with putting the pieces in their appropriate places, the skill of seeing relationships can also be encouraged. "Why do you think the balloons go there?" "Because the girl is holding the strings they go on!" may be the delighted response of the child.

Learning new words, matching shapes, seeing differences, and learning "what goes with what" ("the balloon goes with the string") are some of the pre-reading skills that the use of good but simple puzzle boards can develop.

*Caution:* Regular jigsaw puzzles are better for older children. The random jigsaw cut pieces don't lend themselves to naming distinct objects. This kind of jigsaw puzzle does encourage matching shapes and sizes—good pre-reading skills, but they are usually too difficult for this age.

## BLOCKS: HELPFUL PLAY MATERIALS

By this age, most young children have been given many playthings. Some are soon discarded, others used infrequently. There are some, however, that children return to again and again. Such favorite play materials usually include large and small blocks. Blocks have a lasting appeal because, in a sense, they are tools—tools with which children can express a variety of ideas, feelings, and new concepts.

### Using Blocks

Preschool groups—nursery school, day-care centers—have long used unit blocks as basic equipment.* These blocks, made of smooth wood, are cut so that all the blocks are

*Unit blocks can be ordered from: Childcraft, 155 E. 23rd St., N.Y. N.Y. 10010.

multiples of, or parts of, a basic rectangular unit block. Children may discover as they play that two half unit blocks are the same size as one unit block.

At home, a smaller set of unit blocks not only helps children make the same discoveries, but helps them understand the look and feeling of what some words mean, such as *square, rectangular, triangle, twice as big, one-half as big*. Children come to understand these abstract mathematical terms because they have been able to learn them in a tangible way.

Jim Moffat talks about his daughter, Erica:

When Erica was three, we bought her some unit blocks. At first, she just pushed them around the floor; or piled them up only to knock them down. Then she used them as simple block beds for her dolls. I began to think the blocks were a waste of time and money.

But as time went on, I saw her continue using the blocks, working on block patterns, matching similar blocks. One day she spent a long time fitting the triangles into two squares, then adding the same size unit block on top. She chattered to herself as she worked on these patterns, and I saw she was conducting some kind of experiment. I saw that she was testing and comparing sizes and shapes. I saw that when she used unit blocks in place of a long block, she was multiplying.

Later she started making houses—just outlines, really—roads, filling stations: one upright block cylinder was the pump. We're seeing her reproduce some of her trip experiences, her favorite story-book plots—in a very simple manner, of course. I never knew blocks could be so adapted to dramatic play.

She's expanding her language and really getting into practical math—and nobody's teaching her. Guess we'll get her some more blocks, maybe a few of the curved ones for her next birthday.

### Practical Considerations

Erica's smoothly sanded, accurately cut and proportioned blocks are expensive to buy; but she won't outgrow them for many years and they won't break, wear out, lose their shape

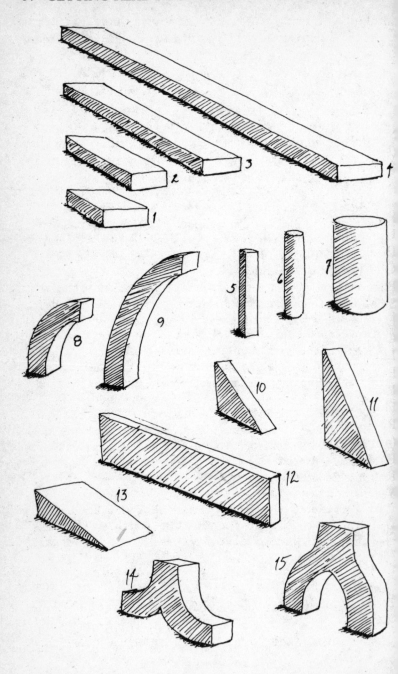

## SUGGESTED EQUIPMENT FOR BLOCK BUILDING

Set of blocks for a group of 15–20 children★
(Numbers in parenthesis refer to drawing.)

|  | 3 Years | 4 Years | 5 years |
|---|---|---|---|
| Half units (1) | 48 | 48 | 60 |
| Units (2) | 108 | 192 | 220 |
| Double units (3) | 96 | 140 | 190 |
| Quadruple units (4) | 48 | 48 | 72 |
| Pillars (5) | 24 | 48 | 72 |
| Small cylinders (6) | 20 | 32 | 40 |
| Large cylinders (7) | 20 | 24 | 32 |
| Circular curves (8) | 12 | 16 | 20 |
| Elliptical curves (9) | 8 | 16 | 20 |
| Pairs of small triangles (10) | 8 | 16 | 18 |
| Pairs of large triangles (11) | 4 | 8 | 12 |
| Floor boards—11″ (12) | 12 | 30 | 60 |
| Roof boards—22″ (not illustrated) | 0 | 12 | 20 |
| Ramps (13) | 12 | 32 | 40 |
| Right angle switches (14) | 0 | 4 | 8 |
| Y switches (15) | 2 | 2 | 4 |

★Jessie Stanton, Alma Weisberg, and the faculty of the Bank Street School for Children, *Play Equipment for the Nursery School* (New York: Bank Street College of Education). Used by permission.

or finish; they can be handed down to Erica's younger brother. Thus, over the years, they will prove much less costly than "the newest toys on the market," which seem to be increasingly complex, costly, and directed toward one use only. Such gadgets may add to older children's electronic mastery, but aren't helpful to the youngest. Even a three-year-old can cause an electronically controlled car to move by pushing a button, but then what? Since the button pushing involves few muscles and little thought, the child isn't learning either through senses or mind.

Compare this static picture with a child like Erica, crawling on the floor, pushing a block on a block road, perhaps murmuring, "Car going to store. Car back up—don't hit curb! Erica put dog in car. Put Meaty Meal [dog food] in car. Car going home—putt, putt. Don't jump out, dog!"

Here, Erica is acting out a part-fantasy/part-reality drama, using her muscles, her imagination, her understanding of daily activities, of vehicle performance. The block is a car in this scene; it will also be used later as a doll bed, as the wall of a house, perhaps as a plateful of "Meaty Meal." Erica is also creating a verbal story. It is randomly constructed, and loosely connected, but it does have sequence, detail, dramatic elements, and a satisfying conclusion. Erica's parent may want to copy it down to read back to Erica's great delight. In fact her mother may be sick of re-reading it long before Erica is tired of hearing it.

Materials that can be used in many different ways, such as blocks, offer the biggest opportunity to children for meaningful play. Block play helps children review and extend their experiences and aids them in discovering concepts fundamental to the reading process. For reading is not just letter or word recognition, it is understanding the meaning behind these symbols. Block play develops not only mathematical concepts but, as Caroline Pratt, the creator of the original unit blocks, said, it also develops "the reasoning out of relationships and drawing conclusions from them"—the bases of thinking itself.

Jerome Bruner, a noted American psychologist, confirms the values of blocks and puzzles as challenging materials for young children. He says that these materials not only help children to establish goals, but offer them the means to reach them: "They can see what they're doing without asking someone."

## OTHER MATERIALS FOR LEARNING

Bruner also feels that children learn through creating their own drawings in much the same way. Drawing and painting are great materials for self-expression, but they also stimulate children's need to explore, discover, make comparisons and distinctions, and develop understanding of the world around them.

### *Paints, Crayons, Paper*

Art materials need not be expensive. Some big pencils and washable Magic Markers are enough to start with. Old newspapers or unprinted newssheets, available at art supply stores, are fine for painting on. A few jars of primary color paints—red, blue, yellow; either dry or liquid—will serve for fingerpainting and brush painting. Old milk cartons cut in half make good receptacles for mixing new colors from the primary colors, an absorbing and satisfying experience for young children. The process itself is similar to later challenges to combine words into new forms or to separate compound words into their basic parts.

*Fingerpaint Recipe*

3 Tbs. cornstarch
3 Tbs. cold water
1 cup boiling water

Mix cornstarch and cold water to paste, then stir in boiling water. Stir until a smooth consistency. Color may be added by using a little tempera paint or vegetable coloring.

Thus, the techniques children begin using in these primary explorations with blocks, puzzles, or paints are the foundations for all learning in the early years. Through first-hand manipulation of raw materials, children develop the mental processes of setting goals, forming judgments, testing theories, changing ideas and plans to meet the goal.

*Wood, Clay, Sand, Water*
Woodwork for twos and young threes isn't usually practical. Most youngsters can't manage the fine art of nailing wood together. They still are happy to bang loudly on a peg-and-hammer set. But clay offers a good opportunity to develop their motor skills (control of fingers and hands) as well as a satisfactory medium for self-expression. Many of their results come from random exploration ("Look! I make cigars!" "I got tails—dogs, fat little dog tails!" "I making worms, squishy worms!"). But some are using this soft pliable material to demonstrate their growing fund of information.

Some three-year-old friends, Jessica, Peter, and Donna, were busily pounding and rolling out Jessica's play dough.

Jessica: Here Goldilocks' chair. Pop! She break chair's leg.

Donna: The Three Bears' bowls. Little bowl, big bowl, big big bowl.

Peter: I got Little Bear's bed. (He smashes it with his fist.) All broke up!

Donna: Soup, soup for bear's bowl. Squishy, squashy soup.

Peter: (Smashes soup.) Soup all on the floor!

Jessica: No, no. Goldy drink soup all up!

Donna: Give it to me—that's my clay!

The three friends fleetingly revealed that they shared a common knowledge: using play dough they recreated some of their impressions. Already Peter wants to change the story to fit his own mood, which breaks up the game. But all have had not only the creative use of materials but also the recall of a shared experience.

*Play Dough Recipe*

1 cup flour
⅓ cup salt
A few drops of vegetable oil
⅓ to ½ cup water

Mix together and add enough water to form dough of the desired consistency. The dough can be colored with vegetable color or a splash of tempera paint.

Sand and water attract young children as magnets attract nails; beaches have always been a favorite arena of activity. We've all seen the contented absorption with which children pour sand and water into containers, over and over again. While much of this play centers on the physical satisfaction these materials offer, a more structural element can be set up, especially in a home setting, if the home can offer either indoor or outdoor space for it. A small sandbox equipped with measuring spoons, cups, and pots helps three-year-olds to discover math properties: this cup holds more than that cup; three cupfuls fill this pot. Initially, a parent or older child can make these observations that help the child make connections such as "three cupfuls fill this pot." Again, raw materials offer possibilities for developing knowledge and motor skills—good preparation for later school success.

*"Scrap" Materials*

Children have always been attracted to bits and pieces of scrounge materials. Their pockets reveal the wide range of their interests: When Paul's mother emptied his pockets, she found two stones, one discarded washer, one bolt, three nails, two squashed berries, a blue jay's feather, and an old broken button.

Collecting and keeping such discards in an empty box or pan can provide young children with materials to use in imaginative ways. Stiff cardboard or other heavy paper provides good background on which children can place and paste these scraps, forming collages. A glue or paste stick is the easiest for small children to use.

Of course, these "found" scraps stimulate children's imagination and creative efforts, but they offer a chance for children to explore the materials' properties also. Learning through their senses as they do, youngsters will come to understand adjectives such as *rough, smooth, round, fluffy*; nouns like *bark, bolt, skin, feather*; and concepts such as *softer than, lighter* or *heavier than*, or *bigger than*. The more first-hand experiences of our world the young child has, the greater the expansion of vocabulary and knowledge—especially under the concerned care of a sympathetic adult.

## PARENT AND CHILD INTERACTION

Though it's been said before, it bears repeating: Children around the world learn best from their parents or the adult in the parenting role. This doesn't mean that these adults actually teach in a formal way. It does mean that children learn to seek and value those things that the parents value and seek.

It also means that the child responds to parental interests. For instance, if parents like to swim, garden, cook, go birding or insect collecting, go to the library, repair cars, or read, their children will most likely be interested, too. Especially if the parents include the child in the activity.

### Talking Together

Children seem to burst forth into fairly complex speech around three, some before this, some when nearer four. Most parents respond delightedly, taking time to answer questions, explain puzzles, converse readily with their child whose steady mastery of language reveals his concepts and misconceptions about the world. Though parents may be amused at a childish interpretation of a common word, they should try not to laugh. Often they are and should be impressed with the child's power to make observations and draw conclusions, as in this incident:

Three-year-old Anne ran up to her father, proudly showing off her new patent leather shoes.

"Wow!" her father said, "those patent leather shoes sure are pretty and shiny."

Anne beamed, then asked, "Daddy, why are they called patent leather?"

Her father shook his head thoughtfully, then admitted, "Gee, I guess I don't know, honey."

Anne squatted down and touched her shoes. After a moment she smiled and said, "I do. Cause they're nice to pat!"

Her father gave her a big bear hug. "You're one smart girl, Anne," he said.

Anne's observation is a good example of the freshness of young children's observations. She interpreted the new words "patent leather" in terms of her own experience, and made a logical conclusion.

Her father also is a good example of a helpful parent; he not only listened to her request, he admitted he didn't know the answer. Sometimes parents feel they mustn't admit to their ignorance for fear of losing the child's respect. Experts say that, far from losing respect, children gain confidence in such an admission. They are comforted to know that adults don't know everything either; and that they, the children, aren't always "low man on the totem pole." At a later age, parents can help children find the answers; right now, Anne doesn't need the actual answer, but is happy to deduce her own original interpretation.

Finally, Anne's father doesn't correct her charming misconception at this time, but warmly—and rightfully—shows his appreciation of her ability to see relationships. Even if her conclusion was faulty, it was based on excellent recall and sharpness of observation.

*Extending Verbal Skills*
Three-year-olds, with new verbal skills, delight in conversation with parents, in being listened to and responded to. All

too often questioning children are ignored or told "Don't bother me now."

They are full of observations about the world, commenting to themselves and others about everything they see. An important shift has taken place. In earlier years, the parent was the talker, the commentator, the storymaker; now, gradually, the child becomes the vocalist eager to use and practice new-found skills, to express fresh ideas.

However, the parent doesn't just listen, doesn't just encourage the child in this very human skill of language. The parent also enlarges the child's vocabulary and comprehension by enlarging the child's experiences; not only by supplying tools for creative play, but by casual question games that can be played in any spare minutes; by exploring the outside world, even if no more than the neighborhood and outside stores; and by reading to the child.

*Exploring the Outside World*

Molly and Matthew are going to the store with Aunt Liz. "Look!" says Matt. "All the people squeezed in that little house there."

"Yes, all squeezed in there," says Molly.

"That's a bus stop shelter," says Aunt Liz. "A place for people to wait. What do you think they are all waiting for?"

"A bus!" Molly shouts.

"A bus," says Matt. "They want a ride."

"How big is a bus?" Aunt Liz asks. "Is it bigger than a car?"

Matt says, "Much bigger than a car. Bigger than Daddy's van."

Molly adds, "Bigger than a horse, big, big, bigger than Amos [their cat]."

This kind of casual questioning helps children not only to use language more accurately, but to sharpen their perception skills; to make comparisons and judgments and see relationships.

As Dorothy Cohen, a noted child development specialist,

has pointed out, to become successful readers children must understand not just how to name and pronounce the letters and words, but must understand the meaning behind them. She goes on to say that to understand this meaning, children must have first-hand experiences with what the word represents, and that the adult's role is to help supply, explain, clarify, or expand those experiences.

This is what Aunt Liz is doing, not as in a formal classroom, but in everyday conversational exchanges. As the children continued on to the store, they stopped to investigate various objects and activities. Sometimes Aunt Liz let them explore by themselves. Sometimes she added a few words of clarification or encouraged them to further thought by her questions.

Does this sound like a lot of trouble? or techniques that only a trained teacher/psychologist/child expert might use?

Absolutely not. It's the natural, normal exchange between caring adults and children. Aunt Liz also pursued her own interests, looking in store windows, checking her money, her shopping list, planning her own activities. Yet she was attuned to the children's activities and could join them when she felt it would be helpful.

What she did *not* do was set a mood of formal "teaching," nor did she decide what they should explore or give them more information than they wanted. As suggested before, she followed their leads and interests, but in a casual manner.

## Many Answers, One Question

Too often, parents (and teachers) encourage children to give only the "right" answer to questions such as "How many toys do you have?" "What is your name?" Of course, knowing the one right answer to such questions is necessary.

But questions should be asked that have more than one answer, for instance, "Can you think of places where people live? or where you think they could live?" "How can people get food?" These kinds of questions help develop perhaps the most important skill we can hope to give our children: the ability to use more than one solution for a question. It's difficult to know what our children's world will be like. But we believe that being able to seek out more than one solution and being literate will provide them with the basic skills for coping with what is now unknown.

This continuing mode of communication and interchange between parent or caregiver and child is a very natural, easy relationship, one that helps develop the child's vocabulary and establishes a method of independent learning: of observation, comparison, examining function, seeing relationships; of asking questions and seeking answers.

*Reading and Questioning*

Questions about a story read to children also help to develop important and basic reading skills. Such questions not only draw children into the reading process, but help them to better understand the text, recall details, make assumptions based on knowledge, interpret character and mood, and begin to predict outcomes.

However, story time mustn't turn into examination time! The aim is not to test the youngster but to help her develop memory and insights. These two suggestions may be helpful:

· Don't ask questions until the child is very familiar with the story.
· Stop if the child doesn't show interest.

Sam Stein read to his daughter Lydia, who was two and three-quarters years old. Sometimes they read favorite nursery rhymes, with Lydia joining in:

Sam:     Hickory Dickory—
Lydia:   Dot!
Sam:     The mouse ran up the clock. The clock struck—
Lydia:   [Holding up one finger]
Sam:     And down he run.
Lydia:   Hittory Dittory Dot!

Another night they looked at Lydia's perennial favorite,

*Goodnight, Moon.* As Sam turns the pages, he asks, "Where's the bunny?"

Lydia: [Silently points to the rabbit in bed.]

Sam: What's he doing in bed?

Lydia: He saying goonight, goonight. Goonight, bear, goonight, chair, old lady.

Sam: What will he do when he's finished saying goodnight?

Lydia: He gotta sleep. Now read it, read it.

As Sam read, Lydia murmured some of the lines to herself.

Sam was wise not to question Lydia further when she wanted to hear the story. Neither did he correct her nursery rhyme pronunciations, nor did he comment on her murmured accompaniment to his reading. Sam's motto, "Easy does it," is a good one to remember with young children.


## SPECIAL TECHNIQUES FOR SHARING READING

Now young children are ready for more language experiences. They can join in "reading" a story they know; they are ready for concept books, which explain activities, relationships, and objects in the world about them. They may also enjoy telling stories themselves, or recalling story details.

### Chanting Refrains

Good books for young children often have catchy refrains. Youngsters not only delight in these rhythmic repetitions, but also often start chanting them. The aware adult will encourage this sharing of the story. Letting children participate so naturally in the reading is a great way to enhance their self-esteem. Sharing the reading also excites their desire to become real readers later on.

Nancy Ragoni's son, three-year-old Marc, wanted stories that allowed him to join in. A favorite story told of a carousel that went "around and around and around." Marc would not only chant the words, but turn around and around himself. (Threes are still learning through body activity.)

Nancy read Marc another of his favorites, *Goldilocks and the Three Bears*. After a second or third reading, she began to pause when one of the familiar refrains occurred; she allowed and encouraged Marc to say the refrain himself. Soon he was eagerly speaking the refrains aloud, even using the kind of voice he thought appropriate: "Someone's been eating *my* porridge," in a deep, husky, Papa Bear growl; or "Somebody's been eating *my* porridge—and eaten it all up!" in a high, squeaky, Baby Bear voice.

Marc responded to the story with all of his senses, as his facial expressions, his gestures, and his voice showed. But even the shyest child will begin to murmur a catchy refrain such as "You can't catch me, I'm the Gingerbread Man," if you will read the story several times and encourage the child's participation. Drawing the very young child into the reading experience in this simple way has proved to be an excellent incentive for mastering reading skills later on.

Also—hopefully—you will still be telling youngsters stories of their own activities. It is easy to insert a repeated phrase into such a story. The phrase doesn't have to be very literary, just easy to remember, as in the following "made-up" story:

Lara tried on a pair of red shoes.
   "Do you want these (red shoes)?" asked the salesperson.
   "No, thank you. I don't want the (red shoes)," said Lara.
   Then Lara tried on a pair of (blue shoes).
   "Do you want these (blue shoes)?" asked the salesperson.
   "No, thank you, I don't want the (blue shoes)," said Lara.

This type of story can continue as long as necessary, ending, of course, in the child's triumphant choice. At first, your child may only want to say the color of the shoes, then gradually join in saying the other repeated phrases. The aim is to help the child share the story with you. Very often, youngsters want to help create the story, too, as they recall the details of the activity—a basic step toward good writing later on. In the small story just recounted, Lara corrected her mother twice: "First I didn't like the *blue* shoes," Lara pointed out. "You said *red* shoes." Later on, she interrupted again. "Tell about how I slip-slid in the black shoes. Tell about the slip-slidey black ones."

Lara not only joined in telling this account of an everyday incident, she also helped to make it. Still later that day, Lara was overheard telling the whole story to her favorite panda bear.

Thus, encouraging a child to take an active part in the reading and telling process in these simple ways—joining in refrains, repeating phrases, identifying colors, names, or order of events—is really important. Let's summarize why:

- It involves the child in saying the written word.
- It helps the child recognize that written symbols represent words.
- It meets the child's desire to enter the grownup activity of reading.
- It meets the child's need to be involved with a loved adult.
- It creates a warm, sociable relationship, which in turn enhances the reading process.
- It creates a feeling of success on the child's part, upon which can be built future reading skills.
- It helps the child recognize sequence of events, recall of details and refrains—all important skills for reading later.
- It encourages the child to branch out on his or her own: adding details, expanding the storyline, telling stories independently of adults.

*Reading Rebus Stories*

A *rebus* story is sprinkled with pictures that take the place of words, like this:

Once a 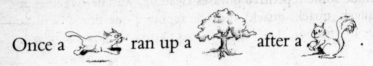 ran up a after a .

Most small children love to "read" the picture at the appropriate time. A good rebus story is truly a shared reading experience. Unfortunately, such stories are not easy to find for this young age; most rebuses are for slightly older children.

For two- and three-year-olds, the rebus pictures must be large enough to be clearly recognizable, with enough details to make them vivid, but not enough to confuse. The story and pictures must be simple enough to engage the child's attention and interest.

If you find such a book, grab it! Your child will really appreciate it and you'll both have fun "reading" together.

*Making Up Your Own Rebus Story*
Since finding suitable rebus stories is difficult, you might consider making your own story. As in making up stories to tell your child, so writing them down follows the same lines:
- a real story about the child's real doings
- a fanciful story about the child's wishes and/or experiences
- a fantasy story about some emotional experience of your child.

What is different about a rebus story, of course, is that pictures replace some words. You will need to think of concrete objects in nearly every sentence so you can represent them in pictures.

Don't worry about your artistic ability: to two- and three-year-olds any pictures, even stick figures, are marvelous, and far beyond their capabilities. They will not be any more critical of your drawing efforts than they were about your singing voice!

Here is an example of a small rebus story centered on the theme of loneliness and making a friend. I also tried to include some repetitive phrases (waddle, waddle, waddle; and quack, quack, quack) and one repeated question, "Will you be my friend?" I added these just to give the child a chance to join in the refrains, if he or she chooses.

Remember, this is only one person's idea of a rebus story: yours will be entirely different, uniquely appropriate to your child. But do try one; you will move not only the least critical audience in the world, but also the most appreciative. And you will be reinforcing that basic reading skill—that words stand for things.

### *Lonely Little Duck*

Little  was all alone.

All alone, little  waddled

through the  .

Waddle, waddle, waddle.

Quack, quack, quack.

Little 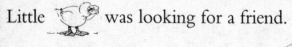 was looking for a friend.

Little 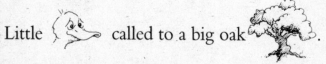 called to a big oak .

"Will you be my friend?"

But the big oak  didn't answer.

A 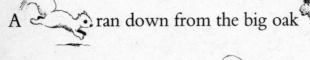 ran down from the big oak .

Little 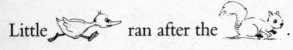 ran after the .

Waddle, waddle, waddle.
Quack, quack, quack.

Little 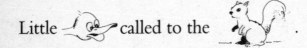 called to the .

"Will you be my friend?"

But the 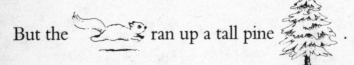 ran up a tall pine .

Little 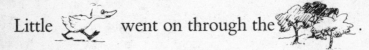 went on through the .

softly crying,

"Waddle, waddle, waddle,

Quack, quack, quack,

Who will be my friend?"

Someone said, "I will."

Little  saw Big  .

"I will be your friend," said Big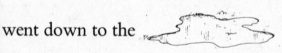

"Come with me."

So Little  and Big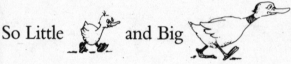

went down to the

Waddle, waddle, waddle

Quack, quack, quack.

In the    were

and

And lots and lots of other  .

"We will *all* be your friends!"

said the  .

So Little was never alone anymore.

Waddle, waddle, waddle,

and quack, quack, quack!

## CONCEPT BOOKS

*ABC's and Number Books*

Sometime during the second and third years, many children become interested in seeing their written names. One way of encouraging this interest is to put their name labels on various items—their clothes, their toys, books, even their special small chair or table.

Parents often spell out the child's name when affixing the labels: "'T-O-M-M-Y,' that says, Tommy; that says your name." Sometimes the child will point to a letter and ask about it, but many children are not yet interested. Again, we follow the child's lead, and don't foist teaching letters until the child is ready.

Usually children become interested in, or exposed to,

ABC books around three years old. The best ones show both the capital and small letters printed in the style that children will use later, like this:

Each letter should be accompanied by pictures that begin with that letter. For example:

A a

At first, the books should be read as "naming books." The adult can say, "A, this is the letter A. All these things begin with the letter A. Can you tell me what they are?"

Some children will be attracted to such books, others will ignore them. It's important to remember not to push these books on the child, but to let him use them or not as he chooses.

The same philosophy is appropriate for number or counting books. Again, look for books that have clear representations of familiar objects beside each number. Let the child name the pictured objects. It's okay if the child also wants to count them, but don't correct the child. For this young age, practicing the names of letters and numbers is enough; they don't have to be said in correct order yet, as such a skill has little meaning to children this young.

Of course, even very young children look at TV programs like "Sesame Street," which emphasize counting and letter naming. Three-year-olds may be able to recite these symbols glibly, and the older children (four to six) have a clearer idea of the relationship between the symbol and the reality, but very young children don't connect the number symbol to objects. And they really aren't ready to do so. It's enough if they grasp the concept that the number symbols represent amounts, and that letters are used to make words such as their names.

The basic mathematical learning still comes from first-hand experiences. Around three, children want and should be allowed to help in household tasks. Of course, they can only do the simplest tasks, but it's well worth the effort to let them. A pattern of household task-sharing is established (however shakily) that will be invaluable later on. Also, there's an obvious opportunity to offer some first-hand math experiences.

Adam Bentley wanted to help set the table. "Okay," his father said. "You can put out the napkins, one for each person. One for Adam, one for Shirley, one for Mommy, one for Daddy. Four napkins, four people." Carefully, Adam put a napkin at each place, saying, "A napkin for Mommy, a napkin for Daddy, a napkin for Shirley, a big napkin for Adam." His father checked them. "One, two, three, four napkins," he counted. "Right you are, Adam. Now put a spoon out for each person. Put one right on each napkin. One, two, three, four napkins—one, two, three, four spoons." "One, two, four, three spoons," said Adam, laying out the spoons.

Though Adam didn't match the symbol name correctly, he did understand the basic concept of numbers. . . . He was beginning to understand one of the purposes of counting.

This practical way of counting is best at Adam's age. Books and television may strengthen his understanding, but only serve as a backup, not as a primary source for teaching.

*Other Concept Books*
There are many books on the market now, covering all kinds of concepts. The best rule of thumb for choosing among them is:

- Choose those that you think would interest or deal with the needs of your child.

- Check for simplicity and clarity of explanation and examples. Are they relevant to your child's experience and level of understanding?

Some of the new concepts the older two-year-old and young three may be interested in exploring are:

- color concepts
- positional concepts (in, out, up, down, under, over)
- size/shape concepts (round, square, rectangular).

Again, television programs, especially "Sesame Street," have presented these concepts many times, so books dealing with the same ideas strengthen the child's grasp of the meaning of these fairly abstract words. (Who has ever seen an "up"? or tasted "rectangular"? or petted a "purple"?) Often, seemingly easy little words, such as *on, in, up, out,* and *into,* prove difficult for beginning readers. A good understanding of abstract words that indicate position, size, shape, and color is a necessary preparation for later success in reading.

One parent wonders why concept books are necessary for kids who have seen such concepts regularly presented on television:

"I'm so bored watching people ask little kids to identify objects shaped like triangles or circles," says Joanne DiMarco. "Why should I overload my son Peter with more of the same in books?"

One answer is that a book allows Peter time to understand these concepts at his own pace. Television's presentations are so fleeting, so quickly erased from the screen, that they also may well be erased from a young child's mind. A book is there to be examined when Peter feels like it. He can concentrate on one part or one image as he wishes. Since Peter will be expected to know some of these concepts when he enters school, why not let him use books to teach himself—perhaps with parental help when needed?

We may feel that the differences between words such as *in*

and *out, under* and *over, in front of* and *in back of* are almost self-evident, but they are brand-new ideas to the twos and threes. Probably the most effective ways for youngsters to understand these concepts are:

· to experience them in concrete ways
· to have us use these terms on everyday occasions and in everyday speech.

What do we mean by these suggestions? Richard Kahn gives us a good example:

My son Robin, just turned three years old, was playing with blocks and small cars. He had placed two blocks upright and laid another across them, forming a small bridge. Up to now, Robin had kept all his blocks flat on the floor; this was a new technique for him.

Making small, motorlike noises, Robin pushed a car under the bridge. I said, "Your car is going under the bridge." Robin repeated my phrase, "Car going *under* the bridge." A few moments later, he was pushing the car over the block connecting the two uprights, saying, "Car *over* the bridge now."

A few days previously, Robin and I had taken a long subway ride. Near the end of our trip, the subway had come out from underground and now traveled above the street on steel girders. Robin seemed confused. He asked, "Train not under now?" I explained, saying that the train had been under the street, now it was going over the street.

Some time later, I found a book about *under* and *over* which I read to Robin. He wanted to hear it twice, but made no comment. When I saw him with the cars and blocks, I realized he was playing out—actually, working out—what his experiences and the book had given him. I guess three-year-olds learn best when they can use real objects, right?

Right, Mr. Kahn. First-hand experience is still best for young children: books and television can explain or strengthen that experience. Until the child has incorporated these abstract ideas into his own first-hand experiences, he has not really learned them.

## LETTING CHILDREN "TELL" STORIES

As most parents know, young children have "read" books to themselves from early on. Hearing a toddler babble as he turns the pages of a well-loved cloth book is a comforting sound to most parents; the toddler is happy, and doesn't need attention. At the two- and three-year-old stages, parents can encourage youngsters in this art of "telling the story" without teaching reading to them. One simple way is to ask questions as the child turns the pages of a book.

Jenny Seul brought a favorite book and sat next to her mother while her mother was reading a newspaper. Mrs. Seul noticed that Jenny was telling the book's story aloud, but in a disjointed way. Mrs. Seul wanted to help without making Jenny self-conscious, spoiling her interest, or trying to teach her.

"Will you tell me about the story, Jen?" Mrs. Seul asked. Jenny began immediately and erratically, saying, "'Bout hen and bad animals. No, no, not me. Who got seed? Bad cat, bad doggie. I do it, I do it."

"Wait a minute; I'm all mixed up," Mrs. Seul said. "Would you start at the beginning, please, Jenny?" Jenny showed that she knew what *beginning* meant by turning to the front of the book. "Who's that?" Mrs. Seul asked, pointing to the picture of a hen. "Little Red Hen," answered Jenny. "And dat de cat, de dog, de piggy."

"What did Little Red Hen ask them to do?" Mrs. Seul went on. "Help plant seed," replied Jenny. "Did they help Little Red Hen?" asked Jenny's mother. Jenny said, "No, no. Not I, not I, not I."

"So what did Little Red Hen do then?"

"Put seed all to herself," shouted Jenny triumphantly. "All *by* herself."

"Then what happened?" Mrs. Seul asked.

In this little episode, Mrs. Seul gently urged Jenny in several ways. Without criticizing Jenny's confused storyline, her mother helped Jenny organize her statements more coherently. Mrs. Seul also helped Jenny to better understand

and state the sequence of events—a very difficult task for young children. By asking, "What happened next? Then what happened?" Mrs. Seul led Jenny from one event to the next. Jenny relished this turnabout of procedure: *she* was "reading" the story to her mother, instead of Mrs. Seul reading it to *her*. With sparkling eyes and eager voice, she answered her mother's questions, pointing to the appropriate pictures.

By recalling the plot, by recounting details and the sequence of events (the storyline), Jenny is imprinting the basic facts of story writing or telling on her mind. Later on, when Jenny writes her own stories, she will understand the format of a story.

Jenny also associates the words in the book with the telling of a story. Her eagerness to repeat the story will serve to help her read later on.

Yet Jenny's mother didn't "teach" Jenny a thing about reading. By helping Jenny recall the story, she helped Jenny to have pleasure with the story, the words, the pictures, and the book.

## WHY NOT TEACH READING ITSELF?

"But why not go ahead and really teach my kid to read the words himself?" asks a father anxious for his son's future success in school. "Won't children be better off learning to read when they show such interest?"

No, not at two or three years old. Now, their main job is developing their skills and their bodies in direct first-hand experiences. If they are deprived of such opportunities, they may well be handicapped later on, as are children with physical or mental problems.

Perhaps this father persists, though less sure. "But isn't that what Mrs. Seul is really doing? Isn't she helping Jenny to read?"

Again, no. Mrs. Seul is helping to straighten out what her child already knows: if there is any "teaching of reading,"

Jenny is doing the teaching herself. And she is doing it through direct, first-hand experience. Most noted experts agree that a formal teaching of secondhand experiences (learning letters, numbers, reading words, etc.) could be actually harmful to very young children; they aren't ready to understand abstract symbols, but are still in what Piaget calls the "concrete" stage, where they learn best through first-hand experiences that they can touch, taste, smell, see. Of course, some young children (usually at least four years old) teach themselves to read. This is okay, as it comes from the child's, not the parents', need. For most of us, the best rule is to "lay off" formal disciplines of reading during these early years.

## OTHER BOOKS FOR TELLING STORIES

There are increasing numbers of wordless picture books published every year; most of these offer excellent opportunities for the child to "read" to his favorite grownup. The first time the adult and child look at the book, the adult may have to tell the story to the child as they turn the pages together. The adult also needs to be alert to any parts of the story or pictures that are confusing to the child.

Bruce Ogden and his son Timmy were looking at a new wordless book about a foolish donkey. The pages were full of busy happenings and objects in Donkey Town, some of which puzzled two-and-a-half-year-old Timmy.

"What that?" he asked, pointing to a barberpole. Mr. Ogden explained, realizing that Timmy hadn't seen a barberpole—indeed, he hadn't seen men shaving with soap, as his father used an electric razor.

Timmy also asked about some of the activities. One that seemed to puzzle him greatly was a painter standing on a scaffold. After trying vainly to explain it, Mr. Ogden said he would show such a painter to Timmy the next time they encountered one in the street.

Bruce Ogden also had to verbally state the storyline, as

Timmy didn't understand at first that the main character's feet (or hooves) were hurting from trying on too-small shoes. In fact, Timmy's father thought the book wasn't too satisfactory, until a week later. Then Timmy brought it to him and proudly "read" it aloud, though he still stated that the scaffold painter was "standing on a step." But by the month's end, Mr. Ogden and his son had seen a real painter on a real scaffold, so now Timmy could "read" the book correctly.

## BOOKS: SPECIAL INTERESTS OF THREES

What kinds of books will appeal to two- and three-year-old children?

Two- and three-year-old children continue their interest in the same subjects that captivated toddlers: animals (real ones, or stuffed); things that move or go; daily or special events; all kinds of people interacting with children; objects in their environment. Now they extend their book interests to match their growing ventures into and curiosity about the world around them. They also delight in more plotted, though still simple, stories, both old and new.

As their social life is being enriched with encounters with adults and, increasingly, with other children, so their concern grows about these contacts. Thus, they are drawn to themes of:

· making friends
· coping with siblings
· coping with parent/child relationships.

Three-year-olds are particularly interested in their own babyhood. They will be attracted to any books about "baby's day"—especially if they can check the pictures with their own history.

Joel Oppers says:

Timothy keeps asking me what he did as a baby. When we hear a baby yelling, he says, "Did I yell, too?" Sometimes he answers himself positively, "No, I didn't yell; I was a *good* baby." He likes to look at baby books, even the *New Mother's*

*Scrap Book*, which is chock-full of all kinds of babies. But most of all he likes to look at his own baby album, and hear about what he did and what we did!

Like Timothy, most three-year-olds like to look at their baby pictures. Maybe they are reassuring themselves of their progress, maybe they are constructing a sense of time: "Once I was like that, now I'm like this; once my parents looked that way, now they look this way." They are establishing an identity, a sense of self, some idea of change and non-change. In fact, they are beginning to deal with very sophisticated concepts that will be with them for a lifetime.

Most three-year-olds, with clearer concepts of time, also enjoy books about the special occasions that highlight the seasons: birthdays, Christmas, Hannukah, Valentine's Day, Easter, summer, fall, winter, spring. Halloween books can be scary to a child who hasn't experienced dressing up; many youngsters are frightened of masks. There are some fairly gentle Halloween books if you think your child is interested. Again, it all depends on the child.

As a three-year-old's understanding of time develops— today, yesterday, tomorrow begin to be meaningful—so, unfortunately, do fears enlarge. Fear of the dark, of monsters, of tigers or bears under the bed, the need for a night light or door left open, may often intensify in the older threes. Comforting adult attention is necessary; but most youngsters respond well to books dealing with these universal states of mind.

## When Twos and Threes Choose a Book

This is a great time to initiate trips to the library. Not only will you be introducing your youngsters to this rich world of books, but they will feel the importance of books to adults and to other children. The children's librarian is a good reference source and can help find the books that will appeal to your two- and three-year-old.

One problem frequently arises: children don't yet understand "returning books" and cling to the ones they choose. As with other problems, if possible follow the child's lead. She can take the same book out again—and again—while you choose another to accompany it. If her allegiance to the original book persists, you may want to buy it for her. But sooner or later, she'll enlarge her "reading" list.

Young children aren't skilled yet in the art of choosing a book. They often just pick up the first one, or blindly grab. In the library, supermarket, or bookstore, it's better to pre-select several books for the child to look at. We want to foster their right to choose while understanding their limited ability to do so. During the more difficult early years (usually at two-and-a-half or three-and-a-half), some young children have trouble making any choice at all. Then it helps to have the adult just take the book, perhaps saying, "Here's a good one; we'll try this," thus avoiding the problem.

## WHAT IS A PICTURE BOOK?

Generally speaking, a picture book is a book for young children in which the text and the pictures are of equal importance. Often the picture is on the page opposite the text. At other times, the art flows through the story. Picture books are meant to be read aloud, so can contain fascinating words.

Picture books range from concept books, counting books, nursery songs and tales, and song books, to folklore, short fantasies, or realistic stories. It can be a "mood" book, which illuminates some human experience or extends a child's insights. We usually think of a picture book, however, as a short, vivid story book, full of (we hope!) good art, short, and simply plotted. Simply plotted, yes—but in no way simplistic. A fine picture book is a work of art.

### The Value of a Good Picture Book
Picture books play a major role in reading readiness. Never again will books make such impressions on our minds as they

did when we were children. Most of us can recall with amazing vividness some story read to us long ago. Thus a good picture book is almost an imperative need—to present to our children the finest art and the best texts to heighten their imaginations and stretch their minds.

Consider *The Tale of Peter Rabbit*, now half a century old: most of us can recall the sight, smell, and taste of Mr. MacGregor's garden; we can remember the shiver of fear for Peter's safety as he frantically tried to escape, and our sigh of relief as the exhausted bunny finally flopped down on the sandy floor of the rabbit hole. I also remember pondering the wise look Peter's mother gave him, though she didn't utter a scolding word. Both that picture and the accompanying text made me wonder: Did some adults act like this? Let you punish yourself for your naughtiness? On the other hand, Mrs. Rabbit *did* give Peter "camomile tea"—what in the world was camomile tea? Whatever it was, I had to assume it was nasty, as the picture showed Peter under the covers, with only his long ears sticking out.

There I was, tentatively exploring new ideas, tasting new words, wondering if Peter's disobedience was worth it, and if I'd go into a Mr. MacGregor's garden of my own. All this questioning, wondering, exploring—just from a simple "story"! That's the affect and effect of a satisfactory picture book on young minds, if they are given the chance to think and ponder, instead of being bombarded by the hurly burly pace of television which allows no time to absorb, sort out, reflect, and wonder.

*What To Look For*

Today many of our best artists and authors also create picture books. They respect their audience, for they know that no audience responds as wholeheartedly. Look for some of the best-known authors and artists such as Rosemary Wells, Evaline Ness, Alice and Martin Provensen, Feodor Rojankovsky, Maurice Sendak, Steven Kellog, Arnold Lobel,

Adrienne Adams, Margaret Wise Brown, and many others; you'll find your own favorites as you browse through the library or a book store.

And as your browse and read, you'll come to realize that a good picture book is very much like good poetry: all extra unnecessary details and words have been pruned away, leaving only the exactly right words. Verbs are vivid, images lively and fresh, and the tone or rhythm of the whole text is just right for that story. And the art extends the thoughts and enhances the words to make the whole story spring to life.

One caution: While picture books were originally intended for preschool children, today the same picture book format is used for much more sophisticated texts for older children—or even for adults. So check the story out for its suitability for your child.

For twos and threes, investing in good, well-made, but inexpensive paperbacks provides the acquisition of old favorites, yet affords to meet the child's growing interests. More expensive but longer-lasting hardcover picture books make delightful "special occasion" gifts.

*How To Choose a Good Picture Book*

We all know our own children's likes and dislikes, their abilities and interests. So we are the best judges of what book will be right for them.

Yet there are some characteristics of good picture books to help us choose the best. Ask yourself the following questions:

· Is the theme—what the story is all about—interesting? Do I agree with it?
· Are the characters believable?
· Do I approve of the values shown in the story?
· Is the story well written? Will I enjoy reading it? Does it have rhythm, refrain, rich language to help our children enlarge their word knowledge?
· Are the pictures clear and simply done to appeal to a young child?

· Do the pictures show interesting details?
· If there are colors, are they bright and clear?

## SOME RECOMMENDED BOOKS FOR THREES AND OLDER TWOS

Three-year-olds, and those approaching three, have a greatly expanded interest in the objects and activities of the world around them. They also have an expanded command of speech, and are eager both to talk and hear about their own doings. Many can recognize some letters—especially letters at the beginning of their own names—and a few numbers, too. They are starting to make more contacts with other children and people, and thus experiencing some of the joys and difficulties in such relationships. They are embarking on the lifelong quest to find out "Who am I?" as well as "Who are you?"

They are still learning best through sensory experiences: therefore, the books that best appeal to their senses will be most successful. As when they were younger, they respond to animals, to rhythmic patterned language, to simple story lines.

Any book list must be only a sampling of the broad array of picture books being published for young children. Also, unfortunately, publishers are taking many books out of print. Thus, some of the suggested books may be available only in libraries.

This list of picture books can be taken as a guidepost for books that are not only appropriate for young children, but have also been approved by children themselves. When you have used some of these books, you'll probably find others with good styles and relevant themes. As always, you are the best judge of your child's tastes and interests.

*Books with Sensory Appeal*
These books not only are about what children can see, feel, touch, or smell, but they also have good texts and excellent art.

*The Noisy Book*, Margaret Wise Brown (Addison Wesley)

*The Quiet Noisy Book*, Margaret Wise Brown (Addison Wesley)

*The Country Noisy Book*, Margaret Wise Brown (Addison Wesley)

> In these noisy books, a small dog (and the listening child) experiences the world through his senses, and has the pleasure of guessing what things are from their sounds, their smells, and their textures. Ms. Brown's lively language, and bright stylized "thirties" art, and the appealing ideas have made these books classics of their kind.

*The Color Kittens*, Margaret Wise Brown (Addison Wesley)

> The words sing, the pictures dance, as the kittens delight in discovering colors. This may well inspire the listener to do the same.

*The Color Bear*, Barbara Brenner (Center for Media Development, Box 203, Little Neck, New York 11363)

*Gilberto and the Wind*, Marie Hall Ets (Viking)

> A young boy plays with and feels the teasing unseen wind; all children, having had this experience, will identify with him—and perhaps express their own feelings about the wind. Striking art.

*The Snowy Day*, Ezra Jack Keats (Viking)

> The sight, taste, touch, and feel of snow is vividly recalled in this bright and beautiful little book.

*Jamberry*, Bruce Degan (Harper)

> Joyful word play about the deliciousness of all kinds of berries.

## Counting, Shape, and ABC Books

Concept books with fine pictures that begin to inform the youngster without requiring feedback. It's best to emphasize these books for picture-naming rather than for letter-learning at this age.

*Count and See*, Tana Hoban (Macmillan)
*Too Many Monkeys, A Counting Rhyme*, Kelly Oeschi (Golden)
*The Berenstain Bears Counting Book*, Stanley and Janice Berenstain (Random)
*One, Two, Three, An Animal Counting Book*, Margaret Wise Brown (Atlantic Monthly)
*Ants Go Marching*, Berniece Freschet (Scribners)
*Shapes*, John Pienkowski (Harvey House)
*An Alphabet Book*, Thomas Matthiesen (Platt)
*Hosie's Alphabet*, Leonard Baskin (Viking)
*ABC Bunny World*, Wanda Gag (Coward)
*The Baby Animal ABC*, Robert Bloomfield (Penguin Paperback)
*An Animal ABC*, Celestino Piatti (Atheneum)

## The World Around Us

Children at this age are beginning to explore the world around them as well as their own familiar setting. They are fascinated by objects in the outside world, both natural (animals, seasonal change, plants, water) and manmade (vehicles, buildings, clothes, objects, books). The short list given here may suggest other books with activities and objects in which your own particular child is interested.

*Over, Under, and Through*, Tana Hoban (Macmillan)
A fresh way of seeing these familiar concepts.
*Look Again*, Tana Hoban (Macmillan)
More fascinating glimpses of bits of objects that will surprise us when we see the whole object from which the bit was taken.
*Green Eyes*, A. Birnbaum (Golden)
Another classic about seasonal change and individual growth with stunning illustrations.
*Things to See*, Thomas Matthiesen (Platt)
One item clearly pictured on each page so child can focus and learn without distraction.

*The Very Hungry Caterpillar*, Eric Carle (World)
  A caterpillar finds out what's good to eat. Stunning
  illustrations.
*Saturday Walk*, Ethel Wright (William R. Scott)
*The Big Red Bus*, Ethel and Leonard Kessler (Doubleday)
*The Big Red Barn*, Margaret Wise Brown (Addison
Wesley)
*The Giant Nursery Book of Things That Go*, George Zaffo
(Grosset and Dunlap)
*My Big Book of Farm Animals*, Jane Carruth (Dutton)
*The Great Big Car and Truck Book*, Richard Scarry
(Golden)
*Big Red Box of Books: Five Picture Book Favorites*
(Random)
  Animal babies—puppies, lambs, etc.—are wonder-
  fully pictured.

## Self-Identity

Young children are already engaged in the life-long process
of learning who and what they are. Though unable to really
comprehend other people's points of view, they are trying to
learn how others act; they are relating their own actions to
the actions of others. Thus, by comparing their own first-
hand experiences to those of others, they are learning both
how much they are alike and how much they are different
from everyone else.

*Everybody Has a House and Everybody Eats*, Mary
McBurney Green (Addison Wesley)
*A House for Everybody*, Betty Miles (Knopf)
*Is This My Dinner?*, Irma S. Black (A. Whitman)
*Be Good, Harry*, Mary Chalmers (Harper)
  A simple clear story of a mother's first leaving.
*The Very Little Boy* and *The Very Little Girl*, Phyllis
Krasilovsky (Doubleday)
  Just right for the very young, but hard to find.
*The BIG Book of Mr. Small*, Lois Lenski (Walck)

This small simple text and pictures of family everyday doings have held children's interests for many years.

*Three To Get Ready*, Betty Boegehold (Harper)

Three wilful kittens discover what happens when they follow their self-centered desires.

*Where Did Josie Go?*, Helen F. Buckley (Lothrop)

Children love to "look" for Josie on each page and to triumphantly discover her at the end.

*Umbrella*, Tara Yoshima (Viking)

Three-year-olds will identify with this three-year-old girl's great love for her new umbrella.

*Are You My Mother?*, P. Eastman (Random)

A bird searches for the right parent.

*Where's My Baby?*, H. A. Rey (Houghton Mifflin)

A different animal baby is hiding behind each folded-over page. Manipulative fun.

*The Snuggle Bunny*, Nancy Jewell (Harper)

A bunny, an old man, and all of us need love.

*The Carrot Seed*, Ruth Kraus (Golden)

A small boy's perseverance wins, despite everyone's doubts.

*Waiting*, Nicki Weiss (Greenwillow)

First separation crisis: a child, waiting for mother's return, lessens her anxiety with gentle activities.

*What's Good for a Three-Year-Old?*, William Cole (Holt)

A collection of poems for the very young.

*Play With Me*, Marie Hall Ets (Viking)

A small girl learns she must consider the needs of others.

*I Am Three*, Louise Fitzhugh (Viking)

The moods and joys of being three.

*Tommy Goes to the Doctor*, Gunilla Wolde (Houghton Mifflin)

*Tommy Takes a Bath*, Gunilla Wolde (Houghton Mifflin)

*This Is Betsy*, Gunilla Wolde (Houghton Mifflin)

*Tommy and Betsy Dress Up*, Gunilla Wolde (Houghton Mifflin)

The charming small Tommy and Betsy books fascinate children right up to school years.

*Good Night, Good Morning*, Helen Oxenbury (Dial)
*Mother's Helper*, Helen Oxenbury (Dial)
*Monkey See, Monkey Do*, Helen Oxenbury (Dial)
*Beach Day*, Helen Oxenbury (Dial)
*Shopping Trip*, Helen Oxenbury (Dial)
Very ordinary, familiar activities that many young children will recognize with Oxenbury's fine illustrations.

*The Golden Egg Book*, Margaret Wise Brown (Golden)
About loneliness and friendship. Very simple, very effective. Try to get the original with its gorgeous art.

*Before You Were Three*, Robie H. Harris and Elizabeth Levy (Delacorte)
This book is written for parents to share with their older children of perhaps six to eight years old. However, the young child will pore over the fine clear photographs of children and babies. It's one of those valuable "buy now, read later" books for both parent and child (as are Brenner's fine books *Bodies* and *Faces* mentioned in the previous book list at the end of Chapter Three, and the equally fine *Oh, Boy, Babies!*, which will be mentioned later).

*When You Were a Baby*, Ann Jones (Greenwillow)
Sometimes, when three-year-olds (and older) want to retreat to babyhood, this may gently remind them of all they can do now.

# CHAPTER
# 5

# *From "Me" to "You and Me": Four- and Five-Year-Olds*

## AN EARLY COMING OF AGE

The small surround of home and family has been the child's world up to now—a comforting, nourishing world that helped to develop his physical, mental, and speech skills. The child has been king of this little family castle; most of his concerns were self-centered.

Though self-interest will still remain at the hub of his concerns, the four- and five-year-olds will become involved with more and more of the world outside the family circle. Now the child's view must be enlarged to include this outside world and the new playmates he will meet there. He must begin the life-long adjustment from "just me" to considering "you and me." This giant step offers new opportunities for expanded reading readiness experiences. The richer the experiences provided by the guiding adult, the sounder will be the learning.

Most four- and five-year-old children bring positive assets to meet this new challenge: their past experiences, the interactions with family members, their secure family position, their new competency with body skills, the growing ability to use materials and language, the eagerness for new knowledge and adventures, and their strong desire for friends.

However, no matter how well-rounded their backgrounds, most children will encounter some difficulties because of their continued self-centeredness, their limited understanding of cause and effect, their lack of social skills, their immature comprehension. Yet, as they move out to meet, play with, and understand other children, four-year-olds and, particularly, five-year-olds develop two important attitudes to bridge the gap between the "me" and the "you/me"—the attitudes of sharing and compromise.

During these years, the expansion of their little world helps children this age to learn more of the system, rules, and order of the adult world, which they practice in their dramatic play and recreate in many ways with materials.

Finally, their growing ability to form friendships and benefit from new experiences is greatly helped by their developed command of language, both from personal exchanges and from listening to stories. Here is where the adult can provide the most direct reading readiness help.

Most fours and fives want to recognize certain words—their own names or the names of a favorite friend or toy, or even favorite foods like pizza. They delight in picking out letters in all kinds of places.

"Look, Mommy," says David (pointing to a DON'T WALK sign), "that's a *D*, just like in *David*!"

Children can use language now to express their feelings, to state their wishes and complaints, to classify and sort out new experiences, and to ask questions. Questions and more questions. "Why?" is the four- and five-year-olds' favorite word.

## "I'M A SEAL GIRL"—A GLIMPSE OF FOUR-YEAR-OLD EMMA

Emma and her parents are at the zoo. Emma keeps up a steady stream of comments and questions; she also is in constant motion: hopping, skipping (with one foot), climbing

on rocks, balancing on the small border fences as they walk
to the seal pool. Emma is entranced by the seals as she climbs
partway up the protective fence. Listen to the conversation
between Emma and her parents:

Emma: That seal is yelling! "Arp Arp Arp!" Why is
    he making that noise?

Father: That's the way seals talk.

Emma: Why do they talk that way?

Mother: Because that's the voice God gave them.

Emma: (Squirming from one place to another)
    What's he saying about?

Father: Maybe he wants his dinner.

Emma: "Arp Arp! Feed me!" Look at that one swim-
    ming. Up, down, up, down, in, out. What
    that seal eat?

Mother: Fish. They eat fish.

Emma: Why?

Father: I guess that's all they find in the ocean where
    seals come from.

Emma: I eat fish too! Arp! Arp! I'm a seal girl! (She
    jumps around barking.)

Mother: (Catching her) Yes, you're my slippery,
    slidey, fishy, barking seal girl.

Emma: Why seals swim up and down?

Father: They like to; that's the way they swim.

Mother: We'd better move on, Fred. It's getting late.

Emma: Why they like to?

Father: That's the way God made them, I guess.

Mother: C'mon, Emma, do you want to see the bears
    before we go?

Emma: No. Want to stay here. (Emma squats down
    and begins printing her name with her finger
    in the dirt. She has the correct letters, but not
    in the correct order, like this: M M E A.)
    Look at me make my name! I can write *seal*,
    too! (Emma draws a backward C and an E
    like this: Ǝ )I'm a seal girl, swimming all

around. (She lies down and slithers over the ground.)

Mother:  (Sighs) Okay, seal girl. But if we stay here we can't see the bears today, Okay?

Emma:  (She has jumped up and is running her hands back and forth across the fence bars) I want to see bears, too!

Father:  Silly Emma, it's time to go now. (He picks her up. Emma yells for a minute. Father puts her down to walk, holding one of her hands as Mother takes the other. Emma hangs onto their hands, lifting her feet off the ground every few steps.)

Emma:  (Singing) Seals, seals in the pool, seals in the sea, see the slippy seals in the sea. (She stops singing.) Is that why they're *seals*, 'cause they live in the *sea*?

Mother:  (With a grin) That's smart thinking, Emma.

Father:  That sure is.

These are the characteristics of Emma, a typical four-year-old:

· full of energy and delight in her physical capabilities
· knowing and using many words to talk to others and to herself
· interested in new ideas, new activities, new games
· eager to extend her knowledge, forming her own conclusions
· eager to venture a little further into the world
· often stubborn, often silly and saucily negative.

## "I'M A RIPPER"—A GLIMPSE OF FIVE-YEAR-OLD MAX

The following is a half-hour observation of a typical five-year-old in his preschool group:

Max was curled over a game of checkers with Rosa. He waved his hands vigorously, shouting, "Move that man, Rosa, then you can double-jump me!"

Quietly, Rosa moved her counter to a position where she could make several jumps. She didn't jump, but neither Max nor Rosa commented on this. Then Max moved his counter, saying, "Watch out! I'm gonna double-jump you!" But Max didn't even single-jump Rosa. In spite of his knowledgeable language, which seemed to be quite advanced for a five-year-old, Max played the game at an appropriately young level— just moving the counter around, shouting directions.

Max and Rosa left the game when Paul, the teacher, called the whole group of children to story time. Max listened to a story about taking care of plants. After the story, Max rushed to a nearby table that had a few small blocks on it. He called to a nearby boy, "Ernest, do you want to be seals or mommy polar bears?"

"A polar bear," Ernest said as he joined Max.

"Good!" Max replied, busily pushing the blocks around. "We're both mommy polar bears."

Paul, the teacher, was sitting nearby. He asked, "Why are the polar bears mommies?"

Holding a block in one hand, Max rushed over to Paul.

"Look," Max pointed out. "There's something on the bottom there. Something like cows have. Both polar bears have these little bump things, so they're mommies."

Then Max returned to his friend Ernest saying, "Lucky thing you're a polar bear. Polar bears eat seals. C'mon, gobble up those seals. Gobble, gobble them up. Some little ducks are passing by. Polar bears don't eat ducks."

In a few minutes he said to Ernest, "C'mon, let's make cards." Max ran to a table where scissors and paper were waiting. He rapidly cut several small, uneven rectangles saying, "Put numbers on them, Ernest." Max then printed an uneven 4 3 4, held it up, and shouted, "Look, almost a thousand!"

Next, he called out, "Cheese, here's some cheese. Here's a hat," as he drew pictures on his cards. He also printed his name on each card with letters in the correct sequence.

Ernest, meantime, had slowly and carefully cut out two fairly straight rectangles, printing a single number on each as well as his name. He held them up to Max, saying, "Here's two cards."

Max kept on working, saying to Ernest, "I might rip them. Don't give them to me; I'm a ripper!"

Rosa came to the table and asked to play. Max answered, "Sure, sure, we need lots of cards."

Paul, the teacher, came over to watch the card-making. Max smiled, showing his cards, naming the pictures and the numbers (some correctly, some incorrectly).

A few minutes later, Max was poring over a brightly colored book. He was talking to Rosa, counting aloud the many balloons on the page.

"Forty-six, forty-seven, forty-eight, forty-nine," Max said. "Whew! A lot of counting!" He turned the page to pictures of more balloons and went on, "ninety-four, ninety-five, one thousand! One thousand balloons!"

This thirty-minute glimpse of Max reveals several characteristics of wonderful five-year-oldness. We can see:

· a general air of cheerful friendliness
· that Max is comfortable playing with one or two children
· that he talks fluently, almost nonstop, as he works
· that the content of his dramatic play changes rapidly
· that he moves quickly from one interest and material to another
· that he can print numbers and letters fairly competently
· that his facile speech seems more mature than his understanding.

Friendly, lively, enthusiastic, competent, full of ideas, on the go—that's five-year-old Max. Like him, five-year-olds delight in their new abilities such as being able to:

· successfully use tools, such as scissors, pencils, crayons
· draw and build more skillfully
· print numbers and letters, recognize words
· work with friends

· dramatize their knowledge
· rush from activity to activity
· try new experiences, create new activities
· and talk!

Above all, to talk! From a wordless babble just a few short years ago, to a seemingly endless flow of words, four- and five-year-olds surely have come a long, long way.

That is, if in their earlier years they have been "bathed in words"; if their fresh enthusiasm, inventiveness and explorations haven't been dulled by formal drilling; if their caretakers have conversed with them, explained to them, read to them, now the results are showing. The youngsters who have not had adults talking to them so lavishly will have fewer verbal skills, and a much smaller vocabulary.

## THE IMPORTANCE OF VERBAL DEVELOPMENT

Why is speaking and possessing a good vocabulary so important? First of all, children are beginning to understand that the printed or written word is "talk written down"; this concept helps greatly in learning to read, in understanding the process. The greater their vocabulary, the more likely they are to recognize a variety of printed words.

Secondly, a large vocabulary helps children express themselves more accurately and in the rhythm and cadence of natural speech. A child who expresses himself in phrases will be able to read phrases instead of word by word. Our language system, with all its beauty of expression as well as its frustrating exceptions, will have been imprinted on his senses. And from listening to many stories, a child will be prepared for the sentence structure: he will expect each piece (or sentence) of the story to say something about a person or object, or to ask a question. He will expect the story to have a beginning, middle, and satisfying end, to move from first page to last, each sentence to be read from left to right. The child with a background of few stories and/or conversations may well be stymied just by the format of printed material.

A third plus for having a rich vocabulary is that it will help the child in his future writing. The child who can write can read. And the child who knows and uses rich language, is enthusiastic about reading and writing, will be a literate person.

## FOR EACH CHILD, A DIFFERENT PACE

Of course, the verbal and physical activity shown by Max may not describe your or my five-year-old; each child develops at his or her own rate. Rosa, for instance, seemed to be shyer, less active physically, and less fluent verbally. Many five-year-olds are slower to form friendships with other children if their previous social experience has been limited. However, Rosa held her own in Max's games and was equally adept in using the crayons and making numbers. Ernest seemed as physically skillful as Max, had a good vocabulary, but was much more deliberate in his work. He was also much quieter.

Yet five is generally a time of great activity and verbal outpouring. This age delights in new experiences, in their own abilities, in their command of language, in extreme behavior. They love or they hate; they love speed and reject waiting. Generally, they are enthusiastic and active. If we think of a child traveling a road from three to five, we will find each of our observed children at a different location on that continuum:

3 YEARS
 · better body control
 · new interests........................... ROSA
 · perfecting new activities.............. ERNEST
 · using language fluently.................. EMMA
 · constant physical energy...................... MAY
5 YEARS
Extremist that he is, five-year-old Max's glibness and flightiness may begin to seem superficial. One way of helping the ceaseless babbler is to listen carefully to what is being

babbled, to pick up one subject of interest and then to zero in on that item. For example, if Max continued his interest in polar bears at home, his parents could deepen this interest by

· suggesting a polar bear book on the next library trip
· reading to Max on this subject
· making a trip to the zoo
· writing down Max's statements on polar bearishness.

This last activity isn't a story but a way to initiate Max's interest in making a story.

This is one way to lead a bright child like Max into deepening and broadening his interests. Paul, the group teacher, probably will develop Max's identification of a "mommy" animal in group discussion, in library book readings, and in personal directive.

However, such adult guidance should be given very gently and subtly. Max's curiosity, his bubbling energy and inventive play, are too valuable to be dampened by constant questions and suggestions. The best method is the one Paul, the teacher, used: to help Max develop his own perceptions and, of course, to keep providing Max and all the other five-year-olds with appropriate materials and experiences for self-learning and growth.

By this time, children have built up a working vocabulary adequate to meet their needs; they are familiar with the alphabet, and are probably able to recite it (thanks to TV shows like "Sesame Street"); they can recognize familiar words in their environments, such as their names, shop and street signs, or ads; they can pick out at least a few alphabet letters, can count to ten or more, can lay out five or more objects correctly. And they have learned all of these basic beginnings on their own without formal teaching.

## WHAT ABOUT YOUR OWN CHILD?

First of all, take an overall view of your child's use of language and counting skills. Do they generally match those of Max or Emma? The matching needn't be too close; your child may be older or younger and certainly different from these two examples.

You might want to use the following suggestions as a help:

Show your child some pictures with some people and/or some animals doing something the child will understand. For instance, one picture might show a child holding a cat and another child holding a dog that is leaping and barking at the cat. The cat's owner may be yelling or crying.

Ask your child to tell you about the picture. Whatever the child says, praise her and encourage her to tell you more. But don't push the child if she shows signs of restlessness.

The following are three typical responses that may indicate not only the child's vocabulary, but her comprehension of the picture.

1) The child *mentions only the people and objects*: "That's a cat, that's a dog, that's a girl." Such a response may indicate the child is seeing the picture as a series of separate items, that she doesn't have the vocabulary to explain the action, or that she is not ready yet to deal with abstractions and implications.

2) The child *offers a simple description of the activity*: "The dog is jumping; the other girl is crying." Such a simple explanation may indicate more command of sentence structure, but still describes the activities as unrelated. Such a response may indicate a need for fuller explanations in everyday conversation to help the child better see relationships.

3) The child *offers explanation based on relationship of pictured activities*: "The dog wants to chase the kitty; the dog's girl is telling him, 'No! Down, doggie!' The cat is very scared. The cat's girl is yelling at the dog, 'Go away! Get out of here!'" Then the child shows she understands and can express the dynamics of the picture's actions in a fluent manner.

Never forget the obvious: for many reasons, your child may be inattentive, bored, sleepy, unwilling, or just having an off day. *Please!* Don't feel you must accept these suggestions (or those in any book) as absolute measuring rods. They are only helpful if they help you and your child.

## What Next?

After you've listened to your child's responses to two or more pictures, you will have some general idea of the youngster's thinking. If you are still uncertain, you can try again with other pictures, or discuss pictures in a child's book.

Let's use, for example, Mrs. Vi Trainor and her four-year-old son, Jamie. His remarks resemble most closely those responses in Answer 2. Jamie recognizes most of the objects in the picture, names most of the actions and objects correctly—though once or twice he points and says "That thing" instead of giving the right word.

Now what? Should Mrs. Trainor try to set up a formal course of teaching words to Jamie?

Of course not! Jamie is developing very naturally, and his mother hasn't any cause to panic or rush to buy workbooks.

What she can do, first, is further observe Jamie's language and ideas in everyday conversations. Then, perhaps, she might decide he would benefit from more specific help in improving his vocabulary and expressing his own conclusions.

## Example A

For example, a shopping trip to the grocery store might provide such an opportunity. Mrs. Trainor may ask her son if he would like this can of chicken soup or that can of tomato soup. If he points at one, rather than names one, she may continue, "Is that the chicken soup? Or is it the tomato soup?" Usually, Jamie will then use the correct name.

If he points at the cherries and calls them strawberries, that's easy to correct. Mrs. Trainor can help him say the right words for her various purchases by asking, "Do you know what this is, Jamie? Yes, it's spaghetti (or an orange, or ketchup)."

————

*Example B*

To help him predict what will happen, his mother just has to be alert for the many opportunities that pop up daily, such as these:

- Jamie has the small can of cinnamon. Mrs. Trainor asks him if he should use the wide or the sprinkle opening on the top; she lets him experiment, and encourages him to express his discoveries in words.
- Jamie has his shoes on the wrong feet. Mrs. Trainor asks him to study the shape of his shoes and feet, and tell her which he thinks match—and why.
- They watch a building being wrecked. Jamie's mother asks him what will happen when that big ball hits the building.

Mrs. Trainor lets Jamie look at a certain number of television shows she feels are suitable for his age. She tries to watch these shows with him, in order not only to judge the show's content but also to ask as well as answer questions about them. She finds TV a great source for helping Jamie predict what will happen next. She asks questions like these:

- The girl put a too-large collar on her dog. What do you think's going to happen?
- What a lot of pie that dog is eating! How do you think he's going to feel?
- If that boy keeps hitting his friends, what do you think they'll do? What will the boy do then?

## TELEVISION AND READING READINESS

Mrs. Trainor is well aware of the attraction television has for her son. Like most parents, she has mixed feelings about TV's impact on children.

What are children learning from television? Is it worth the loss of time that could be used for dramatic play, physical exercise, and reading readiness activities? What effect will such passivity have on a youngster's preparation for school or on the school-age child? Do the possible benefits of television viewing outweigh the possible liabilities?

Many studies have been made and much written on this subject; here, we'll look only at some of the effects of television on the pre-schooler and how it affects his preparation for reading.

## THE PLUS SIDE OF TV

*Enlarging Word Power*

Two small girls are sitting in front of the television set watching a family show. The commercials come on. As the actors speak their lines or sing a jingle, the four-year-old girls join in. They know the lines, word for word.

> "*Amazing*, it's amazing!
> It washes all my clothes so amazingly clean
> Amazing, how you'll shout *Amazing*!
> You're the best cleaner I have ever seen!"
>                          or
> "Purples, pinks, blacks, or reds
> Whites, oranges, yellows, greens,
> Everybody just *adores*
> our delicious jelly beans!"

These particular scenes and the ads are invented; but the ability of the youngsters to repeat any of the commercials' words is very real—as any parent knows! While we may regret the inanity of many commercial messages, we have to admit that they have added a great many words to our children's vocabularies. One of the girls in the above anecdote might well call her mud pies "amazing" instead of "okay" or "nice"; and the other child might murmur to her Grandma, "I *adore* my *delicious* grandma!" If gratified Grandma gushes, "How does that dear child know such big words?" older brother may reply, "No sweat, Grandma! The tube's teaching her."

Yes, the tube is teaching her, no doubt about it. Young children quickly pick up the language of commercials; for better or worse, the tube's language becomes their language. If some parents view this with alarm, they may well consider the plus side: their children are constantly enlarging their vocabulary picking up the skill of putting words together to communicate better. And when the television "teaching tool" is in the skilled hands of a group like Children's Television Workshop (CTW), young viewers may show a growing command of language.

### Increasing Counting and Alphabet Skills

The aim of "Sesame Street," perhaps the best known of the Children's Television Workshop programs, and now showing in many countries, is to prepare young children for competency in reading and math. Shows emphasize learning the alphabet and counting, along with some relevant concepts. "Sesame Street" borrows its rapid-fire jazzy format in presenting both numbers and the letters of the alphabet from commercial advertising. The educators of CTW were well aware of the children's ability to memorize slogans, trade names, and jingles from the fast-paced commercials. "The Electric Company," another CTW production, concentrates on word formation, word rhyming, and spelling. While it is aimed at children in early school grades, preschoolers watch it too. Originally, "Sesame Street" and its "Electric Company" companion were focused on helping youngsters who lacked, to one degree or another, the reading readiness preparation of more fortunate children. These shows offered a kind of electronic Head Start program. Of course, children of various ages and from all kinds of backgrounds watch the shows. There is strong evidence that the rote drills of counting and reciting the alphabet, as well as some recognition of "word families" (cat, hat, bat), and number concepts (the number of four apples stays constant, no matter how the apples are placed) have been well learned by the viewing preschoolers.

However, the relationship of words to books is missing; books are seldom seen, and aren't sold in the one store on "Sesame Street"; nor are people seen absorbed in or excited by reading a book. For all the emphasis on words and letters, there is little emphasis on the end result of putting words together to make a story, a poem, to offer ideas or information—in other words, to make a book.

### Enriching Pretend Play

A preschooler's day is full of dramatic play; she acts out what she has experienced with her toys, her blocks, her "dressing up", or playing with one or two favored friends. The vivid impact of television characters is evident in the play of children who view shows regularly. When Superman flew onto the TV screen, he became an immediate favorite; "small fry" still stalk down the street wearing Superman outfits. A character like this represents the powerful, magical "big guy" that almost all youngsters would like to be. Just as children identify with the hero of a story, they identify with the super heroes on television. They even identify with the power of cartoon characters such as Pacman or Ms. Pacman.

A small group of four- and five-year-olds were busy crayoning in the playpark. Listening to their conversation, I overheard these remarks:

"Pacman wears hats like flowerpots."

"No, Pacman doesn't wear hats, he hasn't any ears."

"Pacman just zips along, snapping them up."

"I'm Ms. Pacman. I'm going to wear a hat."

The last speaker carefully tore a hole in her paper, and placed the paper on her head. Then she ran around calling, "You can't catch me, I'll eat you up." The other children tore after her. One boy called out, "You can't eat me. I'm Oscar the Grouch. I'll grouch you!"

Violent? Unreal? Or are the children getting rid of some hostile feelings in an acceptable way? They weren't acting out any real experiences they'd had, but they were mutually sharing a television fantasy experience. The omnipresence of television, the almost universal experience of children's seeing the same show, is bound to affect their play. What of the child who doesn't see—or isn't allowed to see—the shows that many of her companions see; would she feel left out of dramatic play such as the above? Parents are faced with such decisions when their children are still very young.

Of course, there are some positive effects in children's play that relate back to their TV viewing. One of the segments in "Sesame Street" stresses cooperation, and this has often carried over into play time. A young parent was amazed when he saw his son and another youngster not only speaking the word but practicing it! He was about to break up their spat over the division of some paints when his son spoke. The stunned father says:

> Paul—my ready-to-hit-'em Paul—suddenly grinned and said, "Hey, let's cooperate, Jessica; you make green paint and I'll make orange paint. Then we'll have two more paints to use." And tough Jessica answered, "Okay, Cooperation, that's what we do."

Another show with positive effects on children's actions and on their play is "Mr. Roger's Neighborhood." A recent study suggests that children who regularly view this show and don't watch a lot of the violent TV programs seem to play more easily and with less friction than those watching more violent shows. These children also incorporated into their play many of the fantasy figures in Mr. Roger's show.

*"Reading" Symbols*
Children recognize many words from their everyday exposure to street signs, cereal boxes and soupcans, and store names. In the same way, they learn to recognize many of the names in TV commercials—only TV familiarizes them with many more words than they are apt to see outside in the street. Not only do they know the logos and symbols of many products and companies, they quickly learn to "read"

the familiar words of the labels shown over and over again on the picture screen. Some aspects of this ability to "read" these symbols distress parents; they feel their small children are too ready to accept the claims made by the advertisers. As the ad people well know, small children will insist on the cookie, the game, the ice cream, or vitamin hawked on their daily shows. But parents can also take heart that one more positive value emerges from the youngster's ability to "read" the words on TV: his reading skills are being strongly enforced by this practice, and his vocabulary is being enlarged. (The word *reading* has been set off by quotation marks in this paragraph to indicate that the child may not recognize the word elsewhere but in this particular setting; he really is doing what the schools call "sight reading"—becoming familiar with the look and shape of a word, rather than knowing its component parts.)

Another aid to reading preparation that TV fosters is the often unrecognized but basically important discipline of sitting still. Too much sitting still isn't desirable for young children; but, as the teacher says, "Unless a kid can sit still and listen to me, he won't get directions, explanations, or hear the story." TV surely keeps a child sitting quietly, for better or for worse. And it also helps him lengthen his span of attention—another necessary prereading skill.

*Some TV-Viewing Guidelines*
Unfortunately, many youngsters are overexposed to television and sit in front of it far too long. Some parents have used it as a baby-sitter—a questionable use. Other parents have banned it entirely.

For most parents who don't want to go that far, here's a reasonable rule of thumb: no more than half an hour of television in one day for four- and five-year-olds. Remember, television watching doesn't have to be a daily habit! Parents should decide on appropriate programs for their preschoolers, and should watch with them whenever possible. This allows for both child and parent to respond to the show with questions, explanations, and other reactions; it also gives parents insights into the child's thinking.

When parents are watching their own TV shows, what about the children? Preschoolers, it is hoped, will be in bed when parents really sit down for any lengthy viewing. But newscasts and some early-evening adult shows that air before dinner, which parents may want to see, are not geared to small children. Such programs too often are filled with the latest war incident, crime, or other disaster. One solution is to establish this as a time for children to play in their rooms, to work at a favorite activity, to help set the table, or to look at a book. If this isn't feasible, perhaps parents can wait for the late-night news. Almost all children are going to be exposed to some adult TV. If the family lifestyle does include allowing young children to watch adult-oriented programs, there is one strong precaution that should be taken: Never allow them to watch alone. Even the worst TV show can be reasonably handled if a sensitive, caring adult is present to answer questions, offer explanations, alleviate fears, and in the final solution use the OFF button when it seems appropriate.

### Television Spinoffs

Again, as all parents know, television has spawned many products in the toy world; Superman, Wonder Woman, Elastic Man, Pacman and his counterpart Ms. Pacman, and Star Treks many characters are only a few of the toy figures that have appeared, along with much additional equipment, in toy stores everywhere. Sometimes such exact copies of television heroes make rather dull playmates; children seem constrained to replay the shows they have seen rather than to use the figures for their own dramatic play. At other times, or when the original plot has been played out, children use these figures just as they utilize any doll to interpret their own imaginative dictates or to act out some of their own needs.

Books are often one of the more positive spinoffs of television shows. Not all the books are of the first quality; but if the child's great interest, say, in Cooky Monster makes her beg for the Cooky Monster book, an important step has been taken. She wants you to read to her about something that interests her. She is seeing books perhaps for the first time as something that can enrich her life, even in this small way. No matter that a lot of these thin paperbacks look junky to you. If they really are junk your child will lose interest in them; but they are stepping stones to better books of more lasting interest. And whether or not they are of much value, they are teaching your child some of the basic points about reading, that is:

- Books have a beginning and an ending.
- You start at the beginning.
- You turn the pages (carefully!) one at a time until you finish at the ending.
- The little black squiggles on each page are words, "talk written down."
- You read these squiggles in lines from left to right. (This needs the reader to move a finger across the page under the words as they are read.)
- Words are bundles of short or long squiggles close together with spaces in between them.

Maybe with these benefits in mind, you will feel more comfortable about buying that Cooky Monster shape book?

## Extending TV Interests Into Real Life

Most parents, concerned about the time children spend in front of the television set, have tried to think of ways to enrich this time. They are also bothered that so much of what is presented on television doesn't reflect the reality of life beyond the TV set.

One way to ease these concerns, especially with younger children, is to try to extend some of the television learning into real life. Here is an example of the process described to me by Sam Malinsky, the father of a four-year-old boy and a five-year-old girl. (The show title has been changed but the process is reported as Sam related it.)

> My kids are fans of a show called "The Tunnel Twins." In this freaky little series, some twins go into a little tunnel each time, to emerge into a magical country where they have these zany adventures. Nothing scary, no violence, but a lot of unreality. Made me kind of uneasy. Then one morning we were shopping and Jayne shouted, "Look! The Tunnel Twins!" A pair of twins were shopping there too. This incident gave me an idea. I began to ask the kids to look for other kinds of "twins"; we discovered that shoes were twins, mittens were twins—Johnny even found some twin cracks in the sidewalk! We began looking for tunnels too; the tunnel under the river we all know—we drive in it when we go to Grandpa's. The kids found tunnels all around the city, even in our house. "Look, water comes out of a tunnel," Jayne said, as she turned on the faucet. Now I'm not so concerned about the fantasy of the TV show; I can relate parts of it to our everyday real world. As a matter of fact, it's really extended our thinking. The kids began to be more actively curious about other facets of our city, to see relationships in objects that seemed different to us at first glance.

Another parent relates how her preschooler "reads" many of the supermarket signs. She says:

> Marybeth goes shopping with me. One day I asked her to get some bread without telling her where it was located. She brought it back quickly: When I asked her how she knew, she said, "Oh, I looked for a sign like the Willowfarm Bread one on television: then I could find it." Soon she was collecting milk, yogurt, crackers, detergent, waxed paper. She could locate several words from television ads on most of the aisle signs. Even if they weren't just like the TV commercial names, she could pick out the parts that showed where all that kind of produce was placed."

Parents may capitalize on young children's ability to memorize labels, signs, and printed material by helping them to find similar words in other situations. Such practice is an excellent way to prepare youngsters for formal reading.

## THE MINUS SIDE OF TV

Many articles and books discuss the negative side effects of lengthy television viewing, for children as well as adults. Our concern is how such viewing affects a child's preparation for reading. Most of the same articles and books agree that short spells of TV watching don't seem to have negative effects; their anxiety—and ours—is for the results of prolonged viewing on the child. Many reports show that kids, even those under school age, spend at least four hours daily watching TV.

*Television, the Time Robber*

Lorrie and Dan Richman looked in the door of the motel room. Their sons, Matt, age six, and Jeff, age four, were sprawled in front of the motel TV.

"Hey, you guys," Dan Richman called. "We're going in the pool—it looks great. Come on!"

"Aw, Dad," Matt whined. "*Clash of the Titans* is on! We want to see it."

"Yeah, we want to see it," echoed Jeff.

"No way!" Lorrie Richman said. "That's a two-hour show at least. And it's not for kids your age anyhow."

"It's good, it's good," insisted Matt, his gaze glued to the screen. "We'll go in the pool later."

"Please, please," his younger brother pleaded. "Matt says all this city comes crashing down!"

Their mother said, "You're not going to waste the whole morning in here."

"Matt, you've already seen this picture!" Don Richman said. "You're sure not going to sit here two hours to see it again. Turn off the set."

"No, no," screamed Matt. "Just let me see a little more! This is a good part!"

"We wanna see it! We wanna see it!" yelled Jeff, stamping his feet.

"Out to the pool," ordered his father, while Lorrie Richman turned off the set.

For a short while the two boys cried and sulked before joining their parents in the pool. Soon they were splashing and smiling.

Paddling enthusiastically, Matt shouted, "Look at me swim, Mom! Look at me, Dad!" while Jeff was being a whale in an Arctic sea.

Does this scene seem familiar? It probably happens daily across the country, in motels, hotels, when out visiting, when at home. As adults we know the often narcotic effect television has on us—how many times have we vowed just to look at one program and found ourselves still staring like a zombie at commercials ninety minutes later? Imagine, then, how strongly TV pulls at a child's senses with its fast pace, its constant noise, its images dancing before small, dazzled eyes. A child needn't even listen or concentrate, but just sit passively.

Listening to reading, on the other hand, is just the opposite. A child needs to concentrate quietly to see not with the outward but with the inward eye, to listen, and to understand.

Without adult help and guidance, small children don't have the strength and experience necessary to withstand TV's hypnotic lure, but might spend far too much time crouched in front of the TV screen—time taken away from developing areas of physical and mental skills, of active exercise, of creative exploration and play so necessary for future success in reading.

*The Television Model of Behavior: Aggressiveness*
Many years ago when home television was as new as home computers are now, I was appalled to see one boy ag-

gressively lift another by the front of his shirt and tie—a still-favored gesture of the television "bad guys." I was afraid that kids were going to copy more of the antisocial attitudes shown on the screen.

Unfortunately, I was right—but not entirely. Most studies show that on the whole many kids do tend to copy hostile attitudes and mannerisms, but the kids who actually act out violent scenes are already in some emotional turmoil.

Obviously, television can act as a model for antisocial behavior. The best antidote for that is to act as Lorrie Richman did: push the OFF button on shows that are obviously violent.

Aside from the moral consideration, which is of greatest importance, violent TV shows have other negative effects that are relevant to reading readiness:

- lack of interest in developing reading skills
- lack of concentration in developing reading skills
- a general "itchiness" and disinterest in other kinds of play or games
- a drive to "act out" hostile behavior, usually in social situations.

## Grumpiness

A small child's nervous and muscular system seems particularly affected by prolonged television watching. Many youngsters act cross and grumpy after a lengthy session before the tube. They seem unable to settle down to any activity requiring concentration or accurate discrimination, such as pre-reading games or puzzles.

A young child's world is one of action in which he is the actor, the investigator, the activist, all of which strengthen and develop his body, his mind, and his curiosity—the conditions that enrich reading readiness.

For the viewer, television is a world of silent passiveness. The action all takes place on the screen. The child can't explore or interact with the screen; only his eyes and ears are bombarded with speeding symbols and loud sounds. Small wonder that he is fretful and cranky when all his natural drives have been put on hold!

### Television People Don't Read

The men and women on television shows are seldom if ever seen reading; neither are there children to be seen "lost" in a book.

Dramatically, this is understandable; someone reading isn't lively action. But the message that may come across to young viewers is that to video families, reading doesn't get a very high rating.

Of course, on a very few shows picture books are read to the preschoolers, the most notable being "Mr. Roger's Neighborhood" and "Captain Kangaroo."

Bruno Bettelheim has criticized American textbooks for failing to portray adults or children enjoying reading. On television, adults and children don't even seem to be *aware* of books. Such lack of modeling must have an unconscious and subtle impact on small children.

## TV AND READING READINESS

We all have been made aware of the negative effects of too much television viewing by articles and books. There is still a great deal of controversy, however, about the subject; no doubt the newer studies will throw more light on it. In the meantime, there are some definite conclusions as to the negative effect of television on preparation for reading.

The swift succession of images, the fast pace of the show, the constant noise may overwhelm the young child's receiving system. Doctors have related increased eye and ear problems to too much television exposure. Parents have found that watching a lot of TV causes fretfulness, irritation, hyperactivity, inability to concentrate, to quietly pursue independent activity, or to listen to a story—all serious deterrents to preparation for reading.

Even such highly touted shows as "Sesame Street" deliberately seek a frenetic quality, which may also produce frenetic children. There are questionable subtle effects on children, such as the place of the children in the show: they take little part in the activities, act as a mostly silent background for the stars (adults and puppets) and seem of as little importance as many children consider themselves. Other repeated actions, such as hitting people with custard pies, or having the pie baker fall downstairs constantly, may indicate a kind of violent humor. And what of the painter who paints letters on people's doors, windows, cakes, even heads? Is he saying that indiscriminate graffiti is okay if one is just practicing letters? What does this indicate to the child viewer?

Perhaps the part of the show that is most highly praised by some educators is the teaching of letters and numbers. After constant watching, a child can recite these with ease and little effort. But does she know what to do with them? She has merely learned them by rote without active participation, such as using blocks or matching objects.

The mental confusion engendered by prolonged exposure to television may well interfere with a child's active preschool learning. Parents, proud of a child's ability to parrot the alphabet, may not take time to realize her real ignorance of letters, aside from their place in the alphabet. Because children retain information so readily from television, we can be fooled into thinking they understand and can use it, and we may thus not encourage them to learn at first hand and from their interest level. The child who pores over a book just read to her, pondering the story, perhaps discovering her initials in the print, figuring out what word goes with what picture, is not only learning at the level of her needs but is learning in depth by her own efforts—important processes for reading readiness that extended television viewing not only cannot give her, but may well interfere with.

## COMPUTERS AND READING READINESS

First came television and now comes the computer, already established in many schools and a familiar sight in many homes. Where does the preschool child fit in the computer explosion?

### Arcade Games

When video games first appeared in amusement arcades, children joyously swarmed to use them; some kids even became instant video-game junkies. Preschool children, however, were only on the edge of this child invasion; they had neither the freedom nor the physical access, nor the seemingly endless coin supply that swelled the pockets of older children.

### Home Computers

Now that similar games have moved into homes and are available to all members of the family, parents face new problems: Should preschool children try the computer games, too? Especially those developed for their age level? Will they help children develop reading readiness and/or other preschool skills? Will computers hasten the reading process? If so, is that good or bad?

At this point, the answers are still coming in, studies are still under way, experiments are still being made. But some conclusions are apparent, namely, that preschool children

- love to push buttons and manipulate levers
- like to play and experiment with the computer in a random fashion
- want to try their older siblings' computer games
- are fascinated with and want to try the existing preschool software—sometimes over and over again.

### Tentative Conclusions: Pro Computer

Some experts—notably those in the computer business—state that very young children can and do benefit from comuter experience, and begin to develop desired computer know-how. They say that computers:

- prepare the child for success in reading and math
- strengthen eye/hand coordination
- promote ability to discriminate, notice details
- lengthen attention spans
- give the child a sense of power and delight in accomplishment.

They go on to describe preschools that have found the computer not only a productive machine for preschool development, but a positive force in preparing for school. They feel that they have barely scratched the surface of all the things a computer can do for preschool children, and suggest that very soon children without computer access may be less school-capable than those who have used the computer at home and in preschool.

## Tentative Conclusions: Anti Computer

Other education experts disagree: they feel that the computer will be another important tool in education, especially when teachers have learned to utilize them in the most productive way, and when better software is available. But they feel there is too much pressure to rush into computer use now for the very young child, without fully understanding what role computers can play. These experts ask the following questions:

- How does using computers better prepare a child for reading than the present practice of using books themselves?
- From what necessary learning activities will time be taken to give to computer exploration?
- Does the present software help the child develop preschool skills? If so, how?
- Is a computer conceived of as an individual teacher for each child?
- Is the use of a computer for developing preschool skills

cost-effective in comparison with using books, three
dimensional materials, individual instructors?

· Is there evidence that computer use may be harmful to
the small child? How does its use affect small-muscle and
eye development? How harmful is the low-level emis
sion of radiation? Is eyestrain an additional hazard?

· What aims do we envision for computer use? simple dril
instruction in math and reading? mere familiarity with
the computer itself? development of reasoning and logic

In contemplating these questions, many experts agree on
these generalizations:

· Not enough research returns are in yet to determine the
pitfalls and pluses of using computers with young chil
dren.

· Young children are eager to work with the computer and
do tend to stay with it for long spans of time; they are
not intimidated by it.

· Many preschool children will be experimenting with
using computers at one time or another.

· The best way for young children to learn is still through
the holistic, first-hand experiential approach, with com
puters taking their proper place in the array of experi
ences.

## Conclusions for Parents

After hearing the pros and cons of using computers with
young children, parents must still make up their own minds
They may well conclude that:

· Computers are here to stay and that, willy-nilly, their
young offspring will be using them to one degree o
another.

· No small child will be "left out," however, if he doesn'
have access to a computer; computers are only accessory
to, not the main part of, preschool learning.

· Computers don't provide a magic answer to reading—o
to any learning.

- Computers may be of benefit in strengthening eye/hand coordination, detail discrimination, following directions, symbol recognition—but so are books and workbooks.
- Software isn't yet fully developed but there are some fairly simple, fairly good games for the under-school-age child; parents should examine the various offerings for the suitability of each to their child's developmental level.
- Computers can't replace first-hand real experiences in real situations that are basic to preschool education; such experiences are not only absolutely necessary in developing a child's mental, emotional, social, and physical growth, but should occupy most of a child's waking hours at the preschool stage.
- Computers may, however, add another dimension to the child's growing powers and, if present, should be available to the child for reasonable lengths of time, on a free choice—the *child's* free choice—basis.

## Avoid the Hysterical Hype

Parents are going to be inundated with ads, with letters, and with TV exhortations to buy not only computers but all kinds of "educational" software. Caregivers will be beseeched, warned, and informed that:

OUR PRESCHOOL SOFTWARE PROGRAMS ALONE GUARANTEE FUTURE SCHOOL SUCCESS FOR YOUR CHILD.

WILL YOUR CHILD FALL BEHIND? OUR PRESCHOOL SOFTWARE WILL KEEP HER AHEAD.

WHY CAN'T JOHNNY READ? BECAUSE HE DIDN'T HAVE OUR PRESCHOOL SOFTWARE PROGRAM.

YOUR CHILD WILL BE DEPRIVED, IF NOT COMPUTER-WISE AT FIVE!

One nursery school boasts in an article that its several computers have "benefited every child." On closer examination, the "benefits" seem to be comprised of "learning quotation marks," recognizing the word "PRINT," recognizing numerals and letters, and drawing a robot—all of which could be accomplished less expensively.

Another article states that computers make wonderful baby-sitters for your preschooler, that he can be entertained endlessly by interacting with the computer rather than passively entertained by a TV show. Sure, children do have more to do—and love doing it—with a computer than with a television set; but the best baby-sitter of all is still a warm, friendly person.

But there's no doubt about it: each family member, including the preschool child, will want to play and work with the computer. But parents or other caretakers must resist the "hype" that surrounds them on all sides, coming from educators as well as computer and software manufacturers. Parents must keep young children's involvement with computers on a playful and limited basis, just as they would any other useful learning tool. Children still pass through the usual developmental stages and need time to explore their needs and pleasures fully at each stage; there's no shortcut to fully developed growth. And similarly, there is no shortcut to a fully rounded preparation for reading that will give your child the skills to read with understanding and pleasure.

What parents can do is supply children at each developmental level with appropriate materials (including computers) and first-hand experiences that meet the needs of that level. Slow and easy does it. And remember that any computer is only as helpful as the person who programmed it is knowledgeable. The very young child still needs a warm, concerned human as his primary teacher.

## LOOKING BACK—AND AHEAD

By the age of five, most children are almost ready to deal with the kind of systems, rules, and order that are necessary for breaking the reading code. They are also moving into that stage of development where they begin to grasp more abstract concepts. For example, very young children don't understand that a pint of water is still a pint of water whether it's poured into a tall skinny container or into a wide low one; because the water rises to a greater height the youngsters believe the tall, thin container holds more water than the low, wide one. As children mature, they realize that in spite of appearances, both containers hold the same amount.

Five-year-olds have absorbed an impressive amount of first-hand knowledge through their interaction with family members and with other people, and through their exploration of many material objects and investigations of their environments. They have accumulated a vast amount of secondhand knowledge from their exposure to books and television. They have also attained good muscular development and eye/hand coordination through their physical activities. Are they now ready for the formal teaching of reading?

While a few children may be ready, most are still in the transition stage. Imagine the building and outfitting of a lovely little sailboat. Is she ready to go after three weeks? One month? As with children, the decision lies with the person in charge—and with the ship itself. Does it list a bit too much? Does it need more or less sail?

In reading, the decision may be made by the child himself as he independently learns to read. But in most instances, the adult must make the decision, based on knowledge of his child's abilities, physical, mental, and emotional. These, rather than age alone, will determine whether or not your child is ready to read.

# CHAPTER
# 6

# *On the Threshold of Reading*

## A TIME OF TRANSITION

Fours and fives are eager skills builders, and most of them are aware that the adults around them possess a special skill they do not yet have: adults read. Even older kids read. Most of the people in the child's world belong to that exclusive club of readers—those who can decipher the squiggles of print in books, papers, magazines, on billboards, and even on TV. Children's natural curiosity, and their eagerness to break the reading code are strong incentives to move from reading readiness to full membership in the society of readers.

This is a time of transition, a time when some fours and fives will start to read of their own accord. But it is also a time when the majority of kids will put the finishing touches on their reading readiness foundations.

I well remember a little scene that took place on my sun porch some time ago. Three five-year-olds, Paul, Justine, and Lara, were gathered there looking at or "reading" from a pile of books. None of the children had been taught reading aside from a general background of strengthening future reading skills. But here was Justine, slowly but accurately reading aloud from P. D. Eastman's zany easy reader, *Go, Dog, Go*:

"The green dog is up," reads Justine. "The yellow dog is down." Lara and Paul stopped turning pages of their own books and stared at Justine. With a frown, Lara turns back to her own book, but Paul keeps listening to Justine. Then Lara begins to "pretend-read," making up a story as she turns the pages of her book. "The boy is going out to smash the monster," she reads loudly. "He flies to Spain in Superman's cape, and squashes them. His mother yells at him but he won't come back. He cuts the monsters into bits."

Paul interrupts. "Don't talk," he says. "I want to hear Justine."

Lara lowers her voice, but goes on "reading" her rambling story in a surly grumble. (Her story of violence and mayhem is typical of this age and stage.)

Paul stands up to look at Justine's book. "Where does it say, 'Go, Dog, Go'?" he asks.

Justine points to a line in the book, and adds, "Look, it says it on the front of the book too." She closes the book and she and Paul look. Then Paul asks, "Wanna play checkers?"

Later in the day, I saw Paul looking intently at Richard Scarry's *The Best Word Book Ever*, in which many of the objects and actions are clearly labeled. At another time, I saw Lara closely examining the book, as if she were studying it. Were she and Paul trying to read? Were they teaching themselves by studying Scarry's labels? Had they felt themselves diminished by Justine's ability to really read? How had Justine learned to read by herself?

I also asked myself what my role should be: Should I try to help Paul and Lara to "really read"? Did Paul's desire to switch gears and play checkers mean that he wasn't ready to concentrate on reading yet? What about Justine? Should I be giving her more specific reading help? Then I calmed down, realizing that all three children were at different stages in this transition period from non-reading to reading. My job was to meet each need at each stage, and to continue to provide an overall foundation for reading skills, just as I had always done, emphasizing one or the other of the three basic areas of help according to each child's need. These three areas offer the best methods of helping children through this transitional period, and are readily useful to all parents and caregivers:

- Area One: informal help that uses activities, conversations, and trips to enrich children's vocabulary, to expand their ideas, and to broaden their knowledge.
- Area Two: formal help with games, puzzles, and use of letters, numbers, and labels.
- Area Three: reading stories aloud, helping children create their own stories and illustration.

## AREA ONE: INFORMAL HELP

In the previous chapter, Paul, the teacher, and Mrs. Trainor, the parent, offered good examples of informal help—the kind of help caring adults naturally have been giving since their children's babyhood. The only difference at this age is that parents can expect a real flowering from their earlier efforts. Through the years they have become more aware of helping, and more alert to their child's needs to learn.

*Around the House*
Oddly enough, we can best help our children by letting them help us. By this age, children usually have been participating in some household chores and independent jobs, such as trying to dress themselves.

By four and five, youngsters are not only eager to work independently, but are better able to do so. Sure, they won't perform a great job—and shouldn't be expected to do so. But the rewards of giving them specific jobs (and inventing new ones) are positive and lasting. Here are just a few of the benefits:

- Children will strengthen their small and large muscle development and coordination.
- They will better understand the structure of and need for household duties.

· They will enlarge their language fund to accommodate new ideas and words.
· They will feel the pride of accomplishment, the joy of having a respected place in family life.
· They will be establishing lifelong habits—habits that would be hard to start forming later.

Don't these sound like fine results from the simple act of making a bed or setting a table? This is the best time to establish chores that will be taken for granted later on. It's worth the time and effort to let young children beat the cake mix, add the milk, count out silverware, dust the furniture, help make their beds. The following scene represents a common occurrence in many households, and shows one way informal support helps to develop skills and vocabulary.

Child:  Can I carry in the big dish now?

Father:  No, the *platter* has to stay in the kitchen. Do you know why?

Child:  Un-unh.

Father:  This big platter is for the turkey. When the turkey is all cooked, we'll put it on the big platter.

Child:  Can I carry in the big platter with the turkey on it?

Father:  No, because it will be very heavy then. But you can carry out this *gravy bowl* when the time comes.

Child:  I love gravy. Put gravy in the bowl now.

Father:  I can't. We can't make gravy until the turkey's all done. Then we'll make gravy from the turkey drippings. But you can put the spoons on the table now. One spoon for each person. Five spoons for five people.

Child:  Don't tell me! I can do it all by myself!

## Answering Questions

Does the previous scene sound too idyllic? Can a father or mother have the time and patience for these explanations?

Of course. This is a common way that parents talk to and explain processes to their young child—kind of "on the wing" as parents bustle about the chore of food preparation.

But the four- and five-year-old often tries the patience of his elders in another way: by asking endless questions. As questioning is a dandy form of learning and springs from a child's needs or confusions, we ought to answer their questions as much as possible. If the list seems endless, however, we can stop it by saying, "That's enough questions for now; I'm getting tired out. If you want to know more, ask me again later."

Does the following scene strike a familiar chord?

Bobby:    Does sheeps have tails?

Mother:   (Using right word without correcting child) Yes, dear. *Sheep* have tails.

Bobby:    Do bears have tails?

Mother:   Sure, bears have little stubby ones.

Bobby:    Do birds have tails?

Mother:   Look at that sparrow, Bobby. See its tail?

Bobby:    (Nodding) Do fish have tails, too?

Mother:   (Tiring) Do they? Look in the fishbowl.

Bobby:    Does bees has tails?

Mother:   (Pausing) No, I don't think bees *have* tails.

Bobby:    Does worms has tails?

Mother:   I don't think worms *have* tails—they look like one long tail to me!

Bobby:    Does mosquitoes has tails? Does ladybugs has tails?

Mother:   (Shaking head) You ask the darndest questions! I never saw a mosquito's or a ladybug's tail. I don't think they have any. We'll have to look in your bug book.

Bobby:    Do *you* have a tail?

Mother:   Oh, Bobby, don't be so silly. You know people don't have tails. And that's enough about tails for now.

Is Bobby just being a pest? Asking questions for the pleasure of talking, or getting attention? Or is he trying to form a concept of categories: fish, birds, and beasts have tails; bugs don't, people don't. Sometimes we may think a child's questions are meant to try our patience. But often, if we listen to what they are asking, we can see a real pattern underlying the seemingly random questions. A good rule of thumb is to answer as many as we think will help the child and for which we have patience and time.

Most parents soon can discriminate between "real" questions and those that are mainly attention-getters. The latter often appear at bedtime: "Mommy, can I go to the bathroom again?" or, "Daddy, I need another glass of water"—or tissue, or a window opened or a door closed.

Most parents soon establish a bedtime routine, so they can say firmly, "You've been to the bathroom, had your water, had your window opened." Thus, they have a reason for refusing such requests—except, of course, when they think the child is feeling scared, insecure, or ill. But sooner or later, they have to firmly end the questioning. Five-year-olds' questions are mainly for information, but they and the younger four-year-old can ramble on and on, in a rather meaningless pattern which the child is too young to know how to stop: his parents must do it for him.

Two points are worth noting: In the recent exchange between Bobby and Mother, several times Mother tells Bobby to seek the answer for himself. Probably without realizing it, she is giving him a *method of research* (go study the object in question) that will be of increasing value to him. She suggests they examine Bobby's bug book for answers to his questions about bug tails. Here she gives him another valid research method: using source materials to find answers. Adults who support their children's groping attempts to form concepts by encouraging such first-hand testing are preparing them not only for reading and school, but for coping more successfully with life. Yet the help Bobby's mother gave him was part of a natural conversation—the daily way parents have always helped children. At other times, caring adults

will give answers when research or first-hand testing is difficult.

*Asking Questions*
Parents can also stimulate children to broaden and deepen
their thinking by asking provocative questions (very dis-
creetly), such as in the following example:

Mr. Huston and his daughter, Pat, were watching the construction of an apartment house.

| | |
|---|---|
| Pat: | That scooper thing is biting the dirt. |
| Mr. H: | Yes, the *shovel* is *scooping* up dirt. Can you see what it does with it? |
| Pat: | It dribbles a lot out. Then it dumps into a truck. |
| Mr. H: | Right. I wonder why they're digging out so much dirt. |
| Pat: | Gotta have a cellar. A deep, deep cellar down under. |
| Mr. H: | A cellar like ours? |
| Pat: | No, bigger. Big for *Mary Anne* to stay in. |
| Mr. H: | (Laughing) Oh, you mean like Mike Mulligan and his steamshovel, Mary Anne (from a book read to Pat). |
| Pat: | Yeah. They are making a big big building. |
| Mr. H: | An apartment house? |
| Pat: | Yeah, 'partment house, or castle house, or a tugboat. |
| Mr. H: | A tugboat! |
| Pat: | (Giggling) I fooled you. |
| Mr. H: | You sure did. Tugboats don't belong in dirt. |
| Pat: | No, in water. |

In this warm little exchange, Pat is extending her understanding of the shovel's job just a little more. But her father
never presses her too much; Pat's joking with him shows her
happy attitude. For some parents, the hardest job would be
*not* to teach, to restrain from explaining the whole con-

struction scheme. Other parents, lost in their own thoughts, may not hear the child's remarks at all.

## Trips to Park or Playground

Many parents take young children to play in parks as a daily routine. There, the city youngster learns to use all his muscles in climbing, swinging, jumping; to develop more keen large-muscle/eye coordination on the monkey bars or in the sandbox. He also begins to develop social relationships—a strong drive with fours and fives. Good peer relationships are necessary for later school success. Playgrounds and parks offer splendid opportunities for fours and fives to learn, practice and hone these social skills.

This age group needs sufficient outlet for its overabundant energy; indoor play may not provide enough release. Five-year-olds especially love to tricycle, try to roller or ice skate, and to run, run, run. This nervous energy is another factor that makes us know that formal teaching of reading with its demands for quiet concentration should not be rushed.

## Taking Relevant Trips

Many years ago the noted educator Caroline Pratt stated her concern that young people no longer have first-hand information about how people's primary needs—for food, clothing, and shelter—are met. In a farm-based society, youngsters gathered eggs, helped make butter and bread, picked vegetables, planted seeds, saw trees cut for cabins, cloth spun at a loom. Today youngsters are cut off from understanding where things come from and how they are made, but trips can help children begin to better understand these primary processes in their environment. The more your child can discover relationships and form conclusions about them, the better he will be prepared for school.

All young children should learn how the three basic human needs—food, clothing, and shelter—are met today. This concept should also be the basis for many of the trips taken where children can observe the way these needs are met.

What kind of trips do children like? Those that are related to their interests and help to broaden their knowledge of their community. Young children are particularly fascinated with basic processes that are full of noise, color, and movement. Trains, boats, cars and trucks, fire engines, policemen on horses, and construction and street machines of all kinds have endless appeal to most fours and fives. For example, a relevant trip might be to a railroad or bus station to watch the activity there, or perhaps to talk to the ticket taker. The trip might be a simple one to the shoe repair shop, the florist, a garage, or to a nearby airport. The basic idea is to enlarge the child's knowledge of the jobs adults perform in the community, of the services needed by the people, and to satisfy curiosity about how things work.

One way to learn of a child's interest is to observe her block or other play. How realistic is the play? What are the gaps in her information? Does she seem confused or misinformed about some function or job?

Lucy Sprague Mitchell, a pioneer in education for young children and the founder of Bank Street College, pointed out that a five-year-old city youngster often put her toy horse to bed and fed it beef and milk even though she had seen pictures of stalls and hay. When the child visited a real stable, her play immediately reflected her new understanding and the satisfaction she had in it.

Another clue comes from the kind of questions a child asks. Does your child seem interested in animals, wild ones as well as pets? Does he talk about one animal frequently? A trip to the zoo is always a welcome one for young children, especially if you limit the trip to just a few of the animals your child is interested in.

Larry Burns remembers taking his children, Gary, age five, and Lisa, age four, for their first visit to the zoo:

Both kids were hung up on bears. Real bears, pretend bears, teddy bears. So we went to see the bears. I resisted the temptation to show them the lions, the elephants, the seals. We were going to limit the trip to bears, so that's what we did. And you know what the kids talked about all the way home and all the next day? They talked about the chipmunk—a little wild chipmunk that kept darting in and out of the cage, stealing the bears' food! But that began to lead to a whole new kind of interest in the bravery of the small: how little things, including kids, coped. We talked and read about "small versus big." The kids even dictated some of their own stories to me; how about that?

Larry Burns learned, like the rest of us, to follow his children's lead and became a learner, too.

A trip to a farm may seem equally exciting to an urban or suburban child. Farms are not always easy to find; perhaps your local school could tell you of one to visit. On longer trips, a time-passing game is to ask the children to keep their eyes open for animals, which usually turn out to be domesticated ones. Larry Burns recalls the time when Gary, then age three, saw his first cow and shouted, "Hey, look at the camel!" To city children, a cow and a camel are equally exotic. These trips extend knowledge and help children make new connections: milk from the farm cow is taken to the bottling plant, then sold in a local store. Helping a child form such connections is an excellent way of giving him lifelong methods of observation.

As has been stated, such processes that are true today may not necessarily be true later on. (Milk, for instance, may be packaged and sold quite differently.) But learning the *method* of looking for connections, of figuring out how things and processes relate to each other is an invaluable aid to success in the future, and to successful reading. Such methods will help your child all through life.

Children's language is the expression of their thinking: the more they know, the greater their vocabulary, their use and understanding of language. The richer their use of language and their comprehension of it, the better will be their reading skills. They will recognize words and understand the meaning behind words—the basic foundation of satisfactory reading. Thus, trips offer more than immediate rewards; they strengthen reading and writing skills.

## AREA TWO: SPECIFIC HELP IN PREPARING FOR READING

*A General Caution*
When we use specific "teaching tools," it's sometimes hard to resist the temptation to overteach—that is, to push on beyond the child's interest or need at that point in our eagerness to open the door to reading.

For instance, consider this interchange between Helena Tompkins and her four-year-old, Jethro:

Jethro: Make a sign for me, Mommy. Have it say "Fire Engine," okay? I'll put it on my fire engine right here.

Helena: Okay. (Spelling aloud as she prints) F-I-R-E E-N-G-I-N-E. Fire Engine.

Jethro: Good. Now make one that says "Firehouse."

Helena: How do you ask me to do something, Jethro?

Jethro: Thanks. I mean, please.

Helena: Right. Here's the firehouse sign. (She spells it aloud.)

Jethro: Thanks, Mommy.

Helena: (After a few minutes) Jethro, do you see the same word in each sign? One word in this sign and in that sign that is the same?

Jethro: (Not very attentive) Yeah.

Helena: I bet you know what the word says, don't you? What does that word say, Jethro?

Jethro: Thank you? I mean, Please?

We may smile at this small incident, but it's a rueful smile. We too have sometimes skipped away from the child's interest and we too have expressed ourselves in less-than-concrete language, to our child's bewilderment. (Notice the numerous repetitions of *that, same, word,* and *what* in Helena's questions; none of these words forms a visual picture in Jethro's mind.) On the basis of Jethro's responses, Helena would be better to wait for him to show more specific interest in recognizing written words.

With this cautionary example in mind, use the following suggestions in moderation. As when answering questions about sex, try to answer just the question asked and not use it as a springboard for giving more information than the child has asked for. Our primary job is to be a reference source and to remember that what a child—or any person—discovers for himself is what he learns best. Follow the child's lead, but try not to push him beyond his immediate need.

*Labeling Skills*

Most parents have been labeling for a long time. They have stenciled or sewn names on their kids' rubbers and shoes, on washcloths and sweaters, and in books and personal belongings. And by doing this, they have been fostering their child's recognition of words. A good way to further reinforce the child's awareness of his own name is to ask if he'd like to have it on any of the following: toybox, book shelf, door, cup, or umbrella. Use this standard school manuscript alphabet:

AaBbCcDdEe

FfGgHhIiJjKk

L l M m N n O o P p

Q q R r S s T t U u

V v W w X x Y y Z z

Most children will suggest other desired labels and will
often want to make their own. They will do best with large
cards or sheets of paper. Drawing a line for their letters to
rest on is helpful. Otherwise, unless they ask for help, it's
best to let them experiment independently.

Sometimes a child will ask more directly, "Show me. I
don't do it right."

Answer, as always, a direct request from your child. First
print her name in fairly large letters, like this:

Then help her move her finger over the letters, beginning
each in the direction indicated by the arrow. In this way the
child's hand-eye coordination is strengthened.

In the next step, the child may trace over your printing
with her own pencil a few times. Finally, she attempts to
write her name independently.

In the above exercise remember:
· to say each letter as you write it
· to ask the child to trace over the printed letter. If she seems too timid to start by herself, say, "Okay, let's do it together."
· to praise the child regardless of the result. Children learn best by succeeding, not by failing.
· to keep in mind that you help your child most when you concentrate on the process, not on the result.

Soon your child may want you to label other items, such as his block building *hospital*, or *ambulance*. Encourage him to trace your printing. This will help him discriminate the different shapes of the letters.


*Verbal Games*
Many games are verbal and don't need any equipment or tools—just you and your child. The skills of listening, following directions, remembering, and alphabetizing are some of the pre-reading skills that can be used in a playful way. They are also great helps at times of boredom or stress, or when you both have to wait and wait: at the doctor's, for a bus, or on a long trip.

You'll probably invent games of your own. The following are only a sampling of the many possible games for developing reading readiness and oral language skills.

THE OPPOSITE GAME (LIKE/UNLIKE) Description: The child guesses words that mean the opposite of words he hears.

Directions: "I'll tell you a word and you tell me the *opposite* of my word."

Example: "If I say *hot*, you would say *cold*. *Cold* is the opposite of *hot*. If I say *big*, what would you say? Yes, *small*."

Action: Continue with more of the same, gradually increasing word difficulty. From comparing *hard/soft* you might go to more abstract things such as *mad/glad*.

Variation: Try to find words that are *alike*; try to find words that are people's *names*.

I SPY  Description: The child guesses an object by its described color, size, shape, and so on.

Directions: "I'll describe something in this room (or bus or street) by its color. See if you can guess it."

Example: "I spy something *blue*. Yes, it's your shirt. Now it's your turn to tell me the color of something you spy and my turn to guess."

Action: Take turns spying and guessing. Try to limit the field of objects to immediate surroundings.

Variations: Gradually add other qualities to the chosen object, such as size or location. Then, when the child is ready, switch to the *initial sound* of objects. ("I see a *b*. Yes, a *bus*.") You can add adjectives and/or adverbs to promote understanding and use of these words in phrases like these: "I see a *huge red* something." "I see something *frisky* and *gray*."

THE RIDDLE GAME  Description: Something—either animal, vegetable, or mineral—is described briefly by some outstanding physical characteristics. If the child has difficulty in guessing, more details may be added. This game strengthens listening skills, an important part of reading success.

Examples: "I'm going to describe an animal. Can you guess what it is? I'm small and gray. I creep softly about at night looking for food. Sometimes I live in the field; sometimes I live in your house. My little whiskers quiver when I smell cheese!"

Action: The child and adult take turns giving and guessing the riddles. Start with riddles as simple as, "I'm an animal and I say 'Meow'!" Then make them increasingly harder.

Variations: For your subject matter, try: TV shows or personalities, toys, story characters, family members, and so on.

I PACKED MY GRANDMOTHER'S TRUNK  Description: The original game is based on the alphabet. Each player must recite, in alphabetical order, all the articles already in Grandmother's trunk, then add a new one beginning with the next letter of the alphabet. For example, the leader says, "I packed my Grandmother's trunk with an *A, apple.*" Then the second player goes on, "I packed my Grandmother's trunk with an *apple* and a *b, bag.*" The next person must remember the *A* and *B* words and add a *C* word, and so on.

With your child, you can limit the game to less than twenty-six items; six or seven (*A* through *G*) seem sufficient to begin with. If the child isn't sure of the alphabet yet, that's okay. The memorizing is important, too. Later, at home, you may play the game with a printed alphabet to guide you. Listening, memorizing, and categorizing skills are strengthened by this game.

Directions: "Let's play a funny game. I'll start it. (Go on to explain game rules.) Okay? I packed my Grandmother's trunk with *a*, an *ape*. Now it's your turn!"

Action: Take alternate turns. If child seems stuck, ask him to repeat list. Help him if he continues to hesitate.

Variations: You can pack the trunk with categories of objects, such as fruit, or toys, or certain colors, and so forth. Encourage your child to create new variations.

SIMON SAYS    This well-known game is particularly good when you have more than one child to entertain.

Description: Give commands to do a variety of actions. Before *most* of them, call out "Simon says," but leave out this phrase occasionally. The child or children obey the order *only* if they hear the words "Simon says" before the command. They are not to perform the command if the leader doesn't say "Simon says." With older children, a person is out if he does the wrong thing (acting out a command not preceeded by "Simon says"). But younger children can just go on playing the game.

The kinds of actions the leader (Simon) asks for should be tempered to fit the occasion. For instance, if the game takes place in the dentist's waiting room, the activities should be limited to finger and arm movements, such as "Simon says: touch your nose; put your hands over your head; touch the floor."

Directions: Explain the game rules to children. Decide

whether children who are "caught" are out of the game.

Action: After you think the child understands the game, let the child play the part of Simon.

Variations: "Simon says: find something that begins with *B*" (or any letter of the alphabet). "Simon says: find all the rectangles you can." In the same way, you can have children discover weights ("heavier than a book"), sizes ("bigger than a book"), etc.

FINISH–THE–RHYME GAME    Try a new twist to the familiar nursery and jingle rhymes your child has been enjoying for some time. Now the skills of recall and sharp listening come into play. Say a nursery rhyme or a well-known jingle, but ask your child to say the last line. Later, ask child to fill in second or third line.

Directions: Leader says, "Remember the poem about little Miss Muffet? If I say the first part, will you say the end?" If child seems shy, say, "Let's say the end together."

Action: Recite poem:

> Little Miss Muffet
> Sat on a tuffet
> Eating her curds and whey;
> Along came a spider
> And sat down beside her
> _____!

Pronounce each word carefully. Accept child's version of last line; if incorrect, just say something like "Wow! You sure know how to finish a poem!" The next time you do that rhyme, *you* give the missing line correctly and let child repeat it after you.

Variation: Let child say the poem while you give the missing line. Use familiar songs, too. Sing them out if possible.

FIND THE PINCHING BUG    The Pinching Bug is a lively game for naming the parts of the body.

Directions: "Let's play the Pinching Bug game. Look out!

The Pinching Bug will land on you! When it does, tell me the part of your body where it lands."

Example:

> Here comes the Pinching Bug
> Flying through the air.
> It lands on (your child's name)
> Right about there!

As you finish, you touch the child and the child names the place you touch. At first, touch her on easy-to-name places, such as the ear, nose, chin. As child catches on, make the landing spots harder for her to name, such as her ankle, wrist, heel.

Variations: Let the child be the Pinching Bug, while you give the correct names. Or, let the Pinching Bug land on other things in the room, such as furniture, objects, books.

*Word-and-Finger Games*
Most of us have been entertaining our children with word-and-finger games since their babyhood. We chanted "This little piggy went to market" as we pinched baby's toes. Or perhaps we clapped baby's hands together as we said, "Pat-a-cake, pat-a-cake, baker's man."

Such touching and chanting games were important for early development of reading readiness. Now the development continues as the child herself does the chanting and the actions, reinforcing skills of hand-coordination, memorizing, following directions, listening, and speaking.

EENTSY-WEENTSY SPIDER    Description: The leader demonstrates with his fingers as he chants this verse: "Eentsy-weentsy spider went up the water spout" (leader is touching index finger of one hand to thumb of other hand alternately, creating the illusion of climbing). "Along came the rain and washed the spider out" (both hands over head, slowly descending, fingers wiggling to indicate rain). "Out came the sun and dried up all the rain" (hitch thumbs together, hands spread flat side-by-side; fingers wiggle to indicate sun's rays). "Eentsy-weentsy spider went up the spout again" (repeat the first action).

Action: Leader encourages child to be the leader.

Variations: Make up suitable hand/arm movements to accompany any variations you might want to invent. The following original ones may give you some fresh ideas:

Little-bittle anty crawled along the wall
Down blew the wind and off he did fall;
He landed on his six legs and away he did crawl, saying,
"I never wanted to go on that wall at all."

Busy-busy beetle walking on a shoe
The shoe kicked the beetle into the morning dew.
The beetle shook himself off and crawled along his way, saying,
"Now I don't have to take another bath today."

WHERE IS THUMBKIN?    Description: Leader and child both hide hands behind backs. As they sing, they bring hands to front and wiggle the fingers they are singing or chanting about. Movements of fingers on one hand are copied by matching finger on the other hand. It's as if the fingers are little puppets bowing to each other. Child repeats Leader's actions and joins in the singing/chanting.

Action: Leader sings, "Where is Thumbkin, where is Thumbkin?" (Leader brings one hand to front and wiggles thumb.) "Here I am! Here I am!" (Leader brings other hand to front and wiggles that thumb.)

First thumb (wiggling): "How are you today, sir?"

Second thumb (wiggling back): "Very well, I thank you!"

First thumb: "Run away!" (Leader puts hand behind back.)

Second thumb: "Run away!" (Leader puts other hand behind back.)

Leader then does same actions and words with each finger

in turn; succeeding fingers are called Pointer, Tall Man, Ring Man, and Pinky.

Variation: Let child act as Leader, while parent copies the action.

## Playing Card Games

Young children are fascinated by the cards used by adults. While most card games are for older years, there are some old favorites that may be just right for four- and five-year-olds, especially in simplified versions. Such games also strengthen the pre-reading skills of matching, understanding categories, and practicing counting comprehension.

JUNIOR RUMMY OR FIND THE TWINS  Description: This game is for two players. Use only the twelve face cards for two players. Say the names of the cards if the children don't know them. Then divide them evenly. Each player matches any two similar cards in his hand—say two kings. They place the matching sets face up in front of them to make "books." Then each player takes a turn asking the other for a card to match one he is holding. This game will be over quite rapidly, but it gives kids a chance to match sets and identify face cards. What seems obvious to us is often baffling to a small child.

Variation: As children become more adept, add more cards to the game.

CONCENTRATION  Description: Two players. Spread all face cards down on table. First child turns up two face cards. If they match, she keeps the pair. If the cards don't match, she must replace them face down in the same place as before. The second player turns up one card. If it matches one that was turned over by the child, the player concentrates on remembering that card, and tries to locate it to make a match. If he matches correctly, he keeps the two cards. Game continues until all face cards are matched.

SOLITAIRE  Directions: Let child sort cards in suits. She can pile them, lay them out in rows, or any decorative patterns she chooses.

If she gets diamonds in with the hearts, ask her to look closely at the symbols. Help her to match them, as you mention their names.

"Yes, hearts are in this pile. The little red spots that look like valentines are hearts; they go in this pile."

"The point-ended red diamonds go in this pile."

Variation: As child becomes accustomed to the cards, ask her to put one suit in numerical order.

"What is the first number when you count? Yes, one. Can you find a red card with just one red heart on it? Yes, put the one-red-heart here. Now find a card with two red hearts. Put the two-red-heart card next to the one-red-heart; right!" And so on up to the ten-spot card.

SLAP JACK   Directions: This game is for two or three players. Reduce a pack of cards to face cards and the twos, threes, and fours. Place reduced pack face down on table. Each player turns over one card. If it is not a jack, another player plays. Slowly, the turned-over pile builds up. If a jack is turned over, the player yells "Slap Jack!" as he slaps the jack. However, the other person may yell and slap the card first. The person who slaps the jack takes all the upturned pile. Sooner or later, one person has most of the cards.

Variation: Try "Slap Queen" and "Slap King."

Caution: In these games, there is no emphasis on winning. Preschoolers cannot be expected to handle this kind of competition. That is why a winner/loser game like the so-called "Old Maid" (now sometimes called "Gorilla" or "Monster" in this less sexist era) isn't appropriate. It is better for each player to get some cards. The adult in charge should slide over the question of who has the *most* cards. Attitude counts: if we emphasize the fun of playing instead of winning or losing, the chances are our youngest children will get more learning and enjoyment from the game.

GO FISH   Description: This game, for two or three players, can be played with playing cards, a bought game, or a homemade one. It resembles Junior Rummy. The game involves matching similar cards; asking another player for a card;

"fishing" or picking up a card from the card pile. (Some of the commercial versions are much more elaborate.)

The amount of cards dealt depends on the card-holding ability of each player. The younger child can only manage four to six cards; the more competent can handle eight to ten.

As in Rummy, the game gives the young child opportunity to discriminate, to sort, to match, to count, to concentrate, to use hands in a new way, to experience social skills.

### Board Games

Most board games are heavily slanted toward winning and losing, but for preschoolers the emphasis should be on just finishing the game. One old favorite of young children is Candyland. Your child will like it too, no doubt, but here again you may want to replace "who gets there first" with "who finishes the game." Other favorites are games like Parcheesi or Uncle Wiggly. Each year a new crop of board games arises, some of which may be suitable for the young child. With all games, the process is more important than the result. Young children love to throw the dice and count out spaces on the board, moving their pieces along them. These are important opportunities to strengthen necessary academic skills. But equally important is the social learning involved: that is, having to sit still for a length of time; having to wait for one's turn; having to accept another child's rights, even to his finishing first. These are essential social learnings for acceptable school behavior—and necessary for learning to read, also.

Many board games on store shelves are listed as educational aids, from toddler's sorting games to the latest sophisticated electronic wonder. And many of these games are appropriate for strengthening reading readiness. When examining the bewildering array, try asking the following:

· Is this game right for the age level of my child?
· Does it help my child to think? to experiment? to use his hands as well as his head?
· Does it require my child to do more than push a button?

(Some button-pushing games are okay, of course; a little magic-making gives any child a feeling of power. But too many electronic gadgets deprive children of the fun of making their own decisions.)

· How well does this game strengthen pre-reading skills?
· Will it emphasize: matching like/unlike? recognizing different sizes and shapes? classifying things? sorting objects into different categories? predicting outcomes? figuring out sequence of events? recalling actions or objects? understanding ideas? discovering parts and wholes? discovering new concepts?
· Most of all, beyond all these positive values, will my child have *fun?*

In our eagerness to prepare our children, we must walk that delicate line between indifference and overconcern, remembering always to follow the child's lead, that what he is interested in and enjoys, he will probably learn.

*Homemade Games*
Homemade games and materials are usually a great success because they are made to fit individual needs and interests, and are the result of personal concern and effort. They can be especially effective in reading readiness by sharpening such skills as sequence, sorting and classifying, and word recognition.

The success of homemade games does not depend on the skill and artistry of the maker, but on the subject matter. However crude or fragile the game, it will serve its purpose if your child—and you—have fun with it. To make the following games you will need some of these materials:

· unlined paper
· felt pens or crayons
· scissors
· index cards, lined or unlined
· old magazines and books for cutting out pictures
· glue stick.

First, you can make your own versions of games we've looked at already—Concentration, Go Fish, Dominoes, even Candyland. For instance, you can draw the characters in a Concentration game, using familiar animals: cats, dogs, birds, etc. Or you can cut out pictures and let the child paste them on index cards.

You can also make up your own games to fit the particular needs of your child. Here are some suggestions, but you will undoubtedly invent others to meet the criteria listed on pages 153 and 154.

SEQUENCE GAMES    You will need four to five cards, each card showing one sequence of a familiar action—undressing, eating cake, building a block tower. Put down the first card face up and say, "What happens next? Find the card that shows what happens next and put it beside my card."

This is a very hard concept for younger children, but fours and fives like to get things in the right order. The secret is to keep the events in a very short time space. For instance, a child jumping into water would be shown in four cards: jumping off a diving board, sailing through the air, splashing into water, swimming away. It's a good idea for the adult to put down the first card, then ask the child, "What happens next?" Even then, confusion may still occur. If your youngster seems bewildered, put the cards away until a later date.

A good way to practice the sequence of events is to ask questions about daily chores, as Dave Wolfe did. Dave says:

Jerry, my four-year-old, was having a terrible time getting the hang of his sequence card game. He recognized their correct order when his older brother, Josh, did them, but really didn't understand what the idea was. So I started asking him about daily happenings.

Me:     What are you doing, Jerry?
Jerry:  I'm brushing my teeth.
Me:     What will you do next?

Jerry:  Go to bed.

Me:  What? And leave your toothbrush on the sink? And get in bed with your clothes on?

Jerry:  No, no. First I put my toothbrush here. Then I take off my shoes.

Me:  Wait a second. Do you leave the toothpaste there?

Jerry:  'Course not. I put on the cap and put it right on there (the shelf). Then I take a drink. Then I take my shoes off.

Me:  Great! That's very clear.

I don't know if being so specific really helped Jerry. But pretty soon he had the sequence-card game under control.

When you make cards showing a sequence of events, Dave Wolfe's tight sequences helps us understand the need for very small pieces of action within each frame.

SORTING AND CLASSIFYING GAMES  These games help children look closely at an object, noticing differences and similarities, matching similar objects. A typical example is: MATCHING FACES GAME  Materials: You will need eight blank index cards and a felt pen. Draw two faces just like each other, one to a card, until you have four pairs of different expressions something like the ones on the opposite page.

Mix up all the cards on the table, then let your child match the faces in each pair. Ask your child to tell you what each expression means, how each card "feels."

WHERE'S MY MOTHER? GAME  This is another example of the kind of "close look" children must take to see differences and similarities.

Materials: You can use pictures cut out of old magazines or work books (perhaps your child can fasten them with a glue stick to some index cards). However, as you will need at least six pictures of mother animals and six of their babies, you may draw them more easily, if not better. The aim is to match each mother to her baby to make a "book." (The mother is on one card, the baby on another.)

Divide the cards, spread your cards face up on the table. Then match the correct mother and baby cards. Your child may ask you for a "baby bear," for instance. This goes on like rummy.

There are many kinds of simple similar games to help children develop this "seeing eye," limited only by your imagination and the child's interest. But they all represent a drill in an important pre-reading skill: seeing how objects look alike or different.

RUBBINGS   Another word activity is the making of word rubbings. As people do in more famous places, your child can make a rubbing of words carved in stone, cement, metal. For instance, "water" is a label often found on lid covers on a sidewalk. As a practice run for larger rubbings, have your child rub a soft lead pencil over a sheet of paper with coins underneath. She will delight in the quick images her rubbing produces, and strengthen her recognition of certain coins.

Material: All the rubber needs is a thin sheet of paper and a soft pencil or charcoal. When the paper has been carefully placed on the word, it is then rubbed hard with the soft pencil until the writing stands out clearly.

*Activity Books*

The supermarkets and stationery stores are full of these pliable paper "workbooks," many of which double as coloring books. Preschool workbooks are usually published in series. Your child will probably enjoy some quiet relaxation with workbooks from *The Scribbler's First Series* (Western Publishing), *The Golden Readiness Series* (Golden Books), *The Dell Home Activity Series* (Dell), or the *Sesame Street* workbooks.

None of them, however, is really a workbook in the sense that it would provide your youngster with a complete program of reading readiness skills. Yet they often offer some reinforcement of certain necessary perceptions, such as:

· looking for like/unlike details
· forming contrast concepts such as over/under, hot/cold, big/little, old/young, and so on

- finding objects with same initial sounds (*h*ouse, *h*at, *h*ill)
- locating hidden objects
- discerning missing parts
- listening to and following directions.

These and other examples of good pre-reading skills that you use with your child are the criteria to use when examining the workbooks.

While we feel that the child may enjoy coloring in the book, and developing his physical controls to "stay inside the lines," we don't advocate using coloring books just for coloring. Blank paper and crayons offer your child a much richer opportunity for self-expression, for communication, for artistic delight, and for conceptualizing his world.

Finally, the books wherein children are asked to find a picture by drawing a line between numbered dots can be surprisingly helpful to youngsters who respond to this task. Mrs. Harmon tells us about her five-year-old daughter Jayne's experience.

I bought her one of these follow-the-dots books when Jayne and I had a long bus ride to Grandma's. I didn't really expect her to devote much time to it; I thought it would help if she just colored in it for a while. To my surprise, she became completely absorbed. She asked my help at one point when she had to discover, or "make," a chicken by drawing a line from dot one to dot fifty. Jayne was stuck on finding twenty-one; in this number did the two come before the one or the one come before the two? I didn't go into the whole base ten system with her; that was far beyond her need or interest. I did point out that twenty began like two, so the two came first—voilà! twenty-one! As I watched her grope onward with her pencil, I realized that Jayne, who could count her numbers glibly, was finding a relationship between the *sound* of and the *look* of a number. Now I'm wondering: does she know what the number means?

Mrs. Harmon glimpsed the difference between what many young children *recite* and what they *understand*. That is why

the next and last area of materials for pre-reading skills is s
important.

## AREA THREE: READING AND CREATING STORIE

*Story Dictating and Book Making*
This is surely one of the most successful ways of preparin
children for reading, yet it is possibly one of the least used
Why? Is it because:

· parents think "bought" material better because it's mad
  by "authorities"?
· parents think preparation for reading means specif
  drills on letter sounds?
· parents believe workbooks to be the best method be
  cause they must be educational?
· parents don't know much about story dictation, how t
  encourage it, or what values it has?

Let's assume the last question is the right one. The firs
three assumptions are based on the idea that magic solution
can be supplied by mysterious somebodies called Educationa
Authorities. While recognized educators certainly offer goo
advice and tested materials for strengthening pre-readin
skills, all of them acknowledge the important role of paren
participation and parent-made materials.

DICTATING STORIES    First, what is meant by dictated sto
ries? Simply, stories that children tell and that you writ
down—at least, you write down the principal statements
ignoring the irrelevant verbiage, as Jake Mario did. Jake tell
us:

> My five-year-old Albert is a dreamy kind of kid. He loves to
> listen to me read a story, but never says anything after. Sure,
> he'll answer my questions, but volunteers zero. Then, by
> chance, I stumbled onto a fascinating project. One day, Al-
> bert asked me to tell him a story; I said I was tired, and *he*
> should tell *me* a story. Boy, did it work! A story poured out
> about Albert sailing around having adventures in his boat.

Wait up, I said. Hold on! Let me write that down! He slowed up and carefully gave me a few lines, which I printed. Then I copied them onto a white cardboard we'd been saving while Albert watched admiringly.

> Albert's Story
> Albert's boat almost bumped a whale!
> It almost bumped a submarine!
> It almost bumped Daddy!
> But it didn't bump anything.
> Albert steered it away.

Albert hung over that story the rest of the day. I could hear him reading it to himself—incorrectly. So I said, See that word? It says *bumped*. Can you find another word like it? Another *bumped*?

Albert did, so I carefully underlined all the *bumped*s in red crayon. Then I asked, Do you see another word that you know? Albert nodded and pointed to his name. Right, I answered. I underlined his name in blue crayon. Look at all the words you know, I said. Can you say them? Again, Albert nodded and carefully read them aloud.

Gee, that's great, I said.

Albert pointed to the first line. "Tell me what that says."

I read to him, moving my finger under the words and lines, and he repeated it. We did the same with all the lines, until Albert could repeat all four. Then he shouted, "I'm reading! Listen to me read!" He was proud as a bug and immediately decorated his story with designs and pictures.

Of course, Albert really wasn't reading, he was memorizing. But—as we said before—it's the process, not the result, that's important for preschoolers. Albert was perfecting some very important reading principles. To wit:

- a recognition that print is a symbol for spoken words
- a recognition that printed words come in little bundles of letters; A-L-B-E-R-T is a different shape and bundle of letters from B-U-M-P-E-D

· a recognition that what one says and thinks can be expressed in words and written down in word symbols.

Jake Mario really began to teach reading to Albert, but veered off into more informal help. While he did teach two words, he didn't persist—which was just as well, in view of Albert's lack of interest in learning what each word meant. Albert had enough pleasure for the time being in memorizing the lines and recognizing a couple of words. And Jake, whether he recognized it or not, took his cue from Albert. Now his son will approach future instruction with happy eagerness. But imagine how turned off Albert might have been if Jake had insisted on his knowing each and every word.

BOOK MAKING   After your child has dictated a story, she may want to keep it in a more permanent form, such as a "book." Encourage her to look carefully at a real book and tell you what it is like. Usually, children will want just a back and front cover. Construction paper (the heavy colored sheets available at stationery stores) makes a satisfactory book.

Point out the title and author's name on a book's front cover, also the design or picture. Most children want these embellishments on their own books.

CONTENT OF STORY   If your child has difficulty in thinking of a story, help her to organize her thoughts. One easy method is to help her recall an incident, step by step, as Dahlia Fahnstock did. She tells us:

> My four-year-old, Mairi Jo, wanted me to write down her story, as I had done for her five-year-old brother, Vance. But she couldn't get started; she giggled and wiggled but didn't seem able to think of anything to say.
>
> "How about telling me what you did at Joannie's house this morning?" I asked her.
>
> Mairi Jo yelled, "We ate chocolate *chimp* cookies."
>
> "Okay, I'll put that down," I said, "like this,"

> Mairi Jo and Joannie ate
> chocolate *chip* cookies.

"What did you do then?" I went on.

Mairi Jo didn't hesitate.

"Joannie's cat ate the crumbs. He ate up *all* of them. Krazy Kat loves cookie crumbs!"

I said, "That's a good cat story. I'll write it down just the way you said."

I did, and Mairi Jo was ecstatic; she kept showing the story and reading it to people until the paper was grimy. I even wrote it over for her and she illustrated it and made it into a book. It was almost a month before she wanted to dictate a new story.

On the other hand Vance, my five-year-old son, tells me more stories than I can write down. I've had to say, "Some stories are for telling, some for writing, just the way Daddy and I sometimes read to you and sometimes tell you a story." It's funny; even though Mairi Jo has only two books to Vance's ten, I believe Mairi Jo's mean more to her.

Dahlia Fahnstock shows us one way of helping a child to organize a story: ask her to recall the sequence of events. Asking the child, "What happened first? What happened next?" not only helps her recall the occasion and organize her story, but strengthens her understanding of sequence of events. Your child also learns to discard irrelevant details by your example. "Vance Fahnstock is a nonstop talker," his mother says. "My problem with him is trying to write down the important details in his flood of words."

READING FROM WRITING   As Vance and his mother pull his story from his spate of words, Vance is learning how to organize the main points in his story; he is also learning to become aware of the main points in the stories he hears.

Both children are learning basic information about the reading process from their involvement in story dictation, such as:

- Stories have beginnings and endings.
- They are told in related sequences.
- They are told in sentences that begin with capital letters and end with another mark (period, question mark, or exclamation point).
- Sentences are read from left to right.
- They usually describe a real or imagined event.
- They are written by people.

All of the above points may seem ridiculously simple to us—doesn't everyone know them? Well, not if you are only four or five years old. Dictating a story and "reading" what you've written imprints these steps more firmly on a child's consciousness than just being told about them later. Why? Because first, the child is the originator, the creator; and second, kids learn better when teaching themselves.

*Playing with Words*

Children of this age have a great curiosity about words and letters. Many parents, if they haven't already been pestered, will begin to hear their children ask, "What does that say, Mommy?" or "Daddy, what's that word?" or "That says 'pizza'!"

Youngsters are experimenting with letters, too, singling out those they recognize in unfamiliar settings.

"Hey, Mom, that's a G! Just like my name begins!" five-year-old Gary says, pointing to the first letter of Giorgio's Restaurant.

Another girl becomes ecstatic as she recognizes that her initials are the same as the popular movie, *E.T.* "Emily Terkell! That's like *E.T.*!" she says happily.

While the children's interest in letters and words is of paramount importance, kindergarten also expects new entrants to know the alphabet—another reason to provide word games now.

ALPHABET LETTERS   Many a parent proudly beams when his youngster can recite the alphabet. Shows like "Sesame Street" emphasize this skill. The preschool years are a good time to learn the ABC's, as children readily memorize at this age. One caution, however: glib recital of these letters in their correct order does *not* mean a child can always recognize a letter by itself.

Some good ways to practice learning the alphabet are by using alphabet books and by making alphabet cards.

ALPHABET BOOKS   These come in two forms: the workbook and the picture book. Both are useful in different ways. The workbook is usually slanted toward older children. So, unless your child is already into reading, it's better to hold off using them until later.

The picture book, however, is a fine experience for the four- and five-year-old child. (A list of some excellent ones is at the end of this chapter.)

ALPHABET CARDS   Alphabet cards are an obvious way of playing with letters. You may buy them or make them. If you cut them out you add an extra bonus: letting your child learn by *feeling* the shapes as well as *seeing* them. And if you use fine sandpaper, the *feeling* element is even more pronounced.

After you've cut the shapes, let your child help you paste them on blank index cards. Next to each letter, draw an object that begins with that letter—A, apple; B, baby; and so on.

We sometimes forget that the *name* of the letter is often different from the *sound* of the letter. For instance, the *name* of "B" is "Bee," but the sound of "B" is "Buh," as in *butter, ball*. It isn't necessary to emphasize this difference with your young word explorers, but by saying the words that begin with each letter, they are already hearing a different sound from the letter's name.

Activity: Help your child lay the cards out in the correct alphabetical order. Ask your child to say the letter and the object that begins with that letter as she lays each one down. Once your child is sure of the names of the letters and their alphabetical order, you can play many games.

Variation: Try "Around Around the House." This game is

more active but, like the previous one, it helps the child begin to distinguish the *sound* of the letter from the *name* of the letter. Encourage your child to match household objects with cards that begin with a letter she knows. She can place a "T" on a *table,* or put a *cup* on a "C" card. The idea is to find something to match every card; Z, Y, and X may well go unmatched. You can take turns to quicken the pace.

FAVORITE WORDS   Materials: same as for the Alphabet Cards game described above.

Procedure: Write the child's favorite words on cards. You can start with his name, or with words from his story. Draw a picture with each word. Use the words that he suggests. Do only two or three words at a time. Let the child read the pictures and words to you.

STREET SYMBOLS   Help your child be aware of words in the world around him: store and street signs, direction signs, and advertisements. Of course, most children have long been pestering their parents to translate these fascinating street symbols!

Now some of these signs can be added to your child's word cards and used in concentration games such as described earlier. "Sesame Street"'s regular emphasis on recognizing street signs has brought them to the attention of most youngsters.

NONSENSE AND RHYMING GAMES   Rhyming seems to come naturally to most children. One way to build this delight in rhyming is to play rhyming games. You say a word, such as *can,* and ask your child to say a word that rhymes with it. The game can go on as long as your child shows interest: "fan, tan, pan." Young children also love to invent nonsense words and syllables. I recall vividly a group of five-year-olds chanting, "Bee-bite-bitty, bee-bite-bitty" over and over, and collapsing with laughter at the sound of the words. This joyous exploration of language is a vital part of language and vocabulary development. Such humorous word and rhyming play sharpens the child's discrimination of letters and sounds, builds vocabulary, and helps the child recognize and develop "word families."

*Making Word Lists and Notes*
If your child is interested, encourage her to make verbal lists. Write down her lists of street signs, store signs, grocery items, favorite games. Or you can list for her what she plans to do that day. You both might chuckle at Toad's list in Arnold Lobel's *Frog and Toad Together* that starts,

> Wake up
> Eat breakfast
> Get dressed
> Go to Frog's House

It also might spark off some ideas on your youngster's part, about lists she could make.

Of course, by this time, you'll have set up some daily chores for your youngster. Now is a good time to list the week's chores for the family in an accessible place. Let your youngster mark off her chores daily. This is a good introduction for understanding the concepts of time, such as calendars.

Finally, a note board is not only a necessity for the whole family, but shows your youngster just how important reading is for everyday affairs. You can leave notes for the preschooler by letting pictures take the place of key words. After explaining the idea, read a typical note together with your child, so he can figure the next one out alone. A note like this might serve as a model:

Dear Danny,

 went in the

to the _____ to buy some _____

Drink your _____ and eat a _____

(I love you)

While you may have to read some of the words for your child, you may also be surprised how much he will figure out for himself. Such a rebus note will be fun for your child, and great pre-reading preparation.

*Read! Read! Read!*
So many word activities have been suggested already, from producing a child's own story to making up relevant word games, a parent may wonder, "Is it necessary to keep on reading to the child, too?"

Yes, indeed, for this activity is still basic to good reading preparation. Fortunately, most parents already have established a habit of reading aloud daily, and most parents enjoy this time with their children. If, by any chance, you haven't set up a regular reading-aloud time, don't hesitate to do so.

*Letting the Child Share*
While we talked about letting your child "share" the reading experience by saying repeated refrains ("Here we go 'round the mulberry bush, the mulberry bush"), by saying the word for the object pictured in rebus stories, now your child may be able to really read a single word here and there, which will boost her ego and strengthen her desire to do more "reading." Be on the lookout to ask her to say those familiar bits of the story. Encourage her to read simple words that appear in balloons over a character's head, as in this example:

Wordless picture books can be more fruitfully used at this age; now, with a firmer command of language, your child can "read" these to you more easily and enjoy the importance of being the reader instead of the listener. And of course, your child will be practicing the skills of turning pages from the front of the book to the back, of "reading" the pictures from left to right.

With these and other picture books, you can broaden the child's understanding by asking questions occasionally, especially when the story is finished.

"Why did Goldilocks run away?"

"How do you think the bears felt?"

"Why wouldn't the Little Red Hen give bread to the others?"

"How would you feel if the other animals wouldn't play? Why?"

Of course, such questions should be scattershot, not lumped together like this. But now is the time for children to begin critically looking at the characters' actions, to try to understand how others feel, how they feel. For reading is not just decoding or figuring out words, but also trying to understand what the author means.

But development by questions, broadening of intellectual range, or skills advancement aside, reading aloud is important for itself. It offers a two-way channel between parent and child through which flow loving concern, physical and emotional bonding, and shared enjoyment. As we said in the beginning, reading to your child is the best method of preparing for his independent reading in the future.

*To Teach? or Not to Teach?*
A parent asks:

> "If four- and five-year-olds are developing such pre-reading skills, why not go the whole way and teach them to read?"

First, no matter how bright a child is, he is still immature; that is to say, he hasn't the experience necessary to fully understand the *content* of reading. To really read means to really understand, not just to decode, or figure out words and letters.

Second, the four- or five-year-old world is one of *action*: the child not only still learns best through first-hand exploration, but needs to do so. Why? So that his physical and mental powers may develop equally to give him the skills necessary for reading. The emphasis should still be on joyous exploration, experimentation, and make-believe play—the child's way of understanding and testing his growing knowledge of the world.

Last of all, what's the hurry? What real difference does it make if a child learns to read at five, six, seven, or even eight? The subtle—and not-so-subtle—pressures we feel for success all along the way, may be unconsciously pressing parents to provide early reading skills for their children. Some parents are influenced by the accomplishments of a friend's child. Other parents feel their children will be better off learning to read before entering school. Yet other parents are aware that teaching reading to preschoolers has been advocated by some educators. But, whether the rush to teach reading to youngsters arises from parental ego or from sincere concern, here's the important point: the child, not the parent, is the one who really makes the decision to read. And, most times, the preschooler still wants to play with words rather than to undergo the discipline of formal learning. The comfort for the disappointed, eager-to-teach parent must be taken from the studies that favor holding off on formal teaching. Children who read later seem to maintain an eagerness and delight in reading not evinced by early learners.

*"Look, Ma, I'm Reading!"*
Marilyn Makin says:

> I agree that kids shouldn't be hurried into learning to read. I didn't teach Marcia, my nine-year-old, nor Walter, my twelve-year-old, to read at all. I guess I'm just a laid-back parent. I did read to them a lot, but figured they'd learn to read when they were ready. It worked, too; both Marcia and Walter are good readers, and didn't have much trouble learning in school. They loved reading, seemed to pick it up quickly.
>
> But Totty, my four-year-old, is another kind of child altogether. She's teaching herself to read already! She's always asking, "What's that say? Is this a *T*? Is that an *X*? What's that word? Does that say *elevator*?" Or "Listen to me read this: 'Jenny was a calico cat. She was shy.'"

I don't want to spoil her love of words, and her keen interest in figuring them out. But I don't know how much or how little to help her. Maybe I'm not doing enough. Should I really begin teaching Totty to read?

Since we try to take our cues from the child, the answer is: *Give Totty all the help she asks for.* That may mean teaching her to read, or just helping her when she's stuck. But, of course, it never means forcing reading on her.

There are various ways of teaching reading. You can help her recognize letters and letter sounds. You can help her find words and/or pictures that begin with one letter sound at a time. You can copy down what she tells you and use that story for word recognition. You can help her make a dictionary, using upper- and lower-case letters, full of pictures that begin with each sound. You can encourage her to add words to the dictionary. She can join you in reading refrains in familiar stories, such as "Not by the hair of my chinny-chin-chin," or "You can't catch me, I'm the Gingerbread Man."

Do these suggestions sound very much like those already given? Reading is a process that extends over many years, and preschoolers vary enormously in their journey along the road to reading. Our job as parents is to support and encourage youngsters, whether they are just beginning to recognize letters or already decoding word meanings.

These are just some suggested ways; you can find books that will suggest many more. The important point is to keep the teaching process a pleasant one, as nearly related to the pattern of other activities as possible.

Some adults become stiff and solemn when approaching the 3 R's, as if these skills could only be attained by super people and super drills. Relax and enjoy! We've been helping our children learn math and word concepts since they were born. The best method of all is to continue in the same way, so that you and your child enjoy the process, and to try to be aware of your child's stage of maturity, not trying to lay all the rules on before she's ready. The child who is relaxed but eager and happy to learn reading stands the best chance of reading well. That means, let your children develop at their own paces, let them enjoy plenty of other good experiences, and let them keep hearing good stories.

## GOOD BOOKS FOR FOURS AND FIVES

An asterisk before a title means that the book is suitable for an older five- or six-year-old. The PB after a publisher's name means Paperback.

*Stories*

    *\*James Will Never Die,* Joanne Oppenheim (Dodd, Mead)

        A younger brother finally gets even with his older brother.

    *Pet Show,* Ezra Jack Keats (Macmillan)

        To children, all pets are beautiful.

    *Whistle for Willie,* Ezra Jack Keats (Puffin, PB)

        The yearning of a small child to attain whistling skill will be recognized by youngsters.

    *I Went For a Walk in the Forest,* Marie Hall Ets (Viking)

        A child's gentle fantasy of leading the forest creatures.

    *Noisy Nancy Norris,* LouAnn Gaeddart (Doubleday)

        Nancy's creative noise isn't always appreciated.

    *Bread and Jam for Francis,* Russell Hoban (Harper)

        In this book—one of a charming series just right for the older four or five—Frances the feisty badger learns what happens when she only eats bread and jam.

    *\* Steffie and Me,* Phyllis Hoffman (Franklin Watts)

        A book for a school-age child, but whose natural dialog and everyday happenings will appeal to the more mature preschooler.

    *\*Do You Have the Time, Lydia?,* Evaline Ness (Dutton)

        An older sister's habit of racing from one interesting

job to another keeps her from remembering the younger sibling's needs. Preschoolers will identify with the young child's hurt feelings.

*I Was So Mad*, Norma Simon (Albert Whitman)
Children identify with the various reasons for getting "so mad."

*Umbrella*, Taro Yashima (Viking)
Momo proudly wears her boots and umbrella to nursery school.

*The Snuggle Bunny*, Nancy Jewell (Harper)
A lonely bunny finds a lonely old man to snuggle up to.

★ *Sophie and Gussie*, Marjorie Weinman Sharmat (Macmillan, PB)
Children will recognize the emotions and feelings in these gentle stories of friendship.

*The Girl on the Yellow Giraffe*, Ronald Himmler (Harper)
A lovely gentle fantasy right on the four- or five-year-old level.

*Betsy's First Day at Nursery School*, Gunilla Wolde (Random)
Like all the Betsy and Tommy books by Ms. Wolde, this tunes in to the fears and joys of preschoolers.

*Good Morning, Chick*, Mirra Ginsberg (Greenwillow)
A simple but charming book well suited to four-year-olds.

*The Golden Egg Book*, Margaret Wise Brown (Golden)
Loneliness ends in friendship. Gorgeous art and simple but moving text makes this an important book for fours and fives.

*The City Noisy Book*, Margaret Wise Brown (Harper Trophy, PB)
A little dog must learn through his senses along with the listening child. The other *Noisy* books are equally lively and engaging to youngsters.

*The Runaway Bunny*, Margaret Wise Brown (Harper Trophy, PB)

The conflicting childhood needs for dependence/independence are shown by the bunny's wishful thinking.

★ *The Dead Bird*, Margaret Wise Brown (Harper Trophy, PB)

A straightforward but poetic account of how children deal with a dead bird they find is beautifully written for children five and older. An excellent first introduction to the concept of death.

*Are You My Mother?*, P. D. Eastman (Random)

A small bird asks the question of many animals. A good "matching" theme for four year olds.

*Little Bear*, Else Holmelund Minarik (Harper)

The first of a series of Little Bear books that have enchanted many children with their childlike feelings and activities.

*Happy Birthday to Me*, Anne and Harlow Rockwell (Macmillan)

Just right for that day most important to the youngest children. Other books in this series are also fine for these small family members.

★ *Will I Have a Friend?*, Miriam Cohen (Macmillan)

A small child's worries about the first day of school are assuaged.

*A Dog I Know*, Barbara Brenner (Harper)

The warm, tender relationship between a child and a dog.

*Throw a Kiss, Harry*, Mary Chalmers (Harper)

An incident in the day of this small cat that will awaken instant response from children.

★ *Pippa Mouse*, Betty Boegehold (Dell, PB)

A small creature acts out the everyday activities, frustrations, and triumphs of youngsters in a series of books.

★ *Alexander and the Terrible, Horrible, No-Good, Very Bad Day*, Judith Viorst (Aladdin, PB)

The older child will understand just how Alexander feels.

*A Child's Goodnight Book,* Margaret Wise Brown (Addison-Wesley)

> Animals and children's bedtime, with evening prayers in lovely prose.

*Even If I Did Something Awful,* Barbara Shook Hazen (Atheneum)

> Even if parents don't like what you did, they still love you. A reassuring message.

*Sarah's Room,* Doris Orgel (Harper)

> A small book that children have cherished for years.

*Mr. Gumpy's Motor Car,* John Burningham (T. Y. Crowell)

> An amusing assortment of animals pile into Mr. Gumpy's car. Also try *Mr. Gumpy's Outing.* (Holt Rinehart)

*The Fire Cat,* Esther Averill (Harper)

> A book to appeal to young activists. Also try Averill's *Jenny* books, about another appealing cat.

*Three Rounds with Rabbit,* William H. Hooks (Lothrop)

> Short, humorous stories that encourage independent thinking.

## Information and Concept Books

★ *The Tremendous Tree Book,* May Garelick and Barbara Brenner (Four Winds)

> A lively introduction that will awaken children's appreciation for those awe-inspiring plants called trees.

★ *Have You Seen Roads?,* Joanne Oppenheim (Addison-Wesley)

> A lively, rhythmic examination of all kinds of roads. Also recommended are the other *Have You Seen* books.

*Is It Hard? Is It Easy?,* Mary McBurney Green (Addison-Wesley)

*Easy or Hard? That's a Good Question!,* Tobi Tobias (Children's Press)

> Two books explore this question in childlike ways.

*Do You Know Colors?*, Katherine Howard (Random, PB)

Inexpensive, with bright, clear colors. Just right for a beginning color-concept book.

*My Hands Can*, Jean Holzenthaler (Dutton)

A wonderfully stimulating glimpse of what one pair of hands can do.

*Hooray for Me!*, Remy Charlip and Lilian Moore (Parents Magazine Press)

An affirmation of self.

*Where Does the Butterfly Go When It Rains?*, May Garelick (Scholastic, PB)

This poetic book encourages questioning.

*Night Animals*, Millicent E. Selsam (Four Winds)

Night activities, animal and human: fast-paced action for the youngest.

*A Kiss Is Round*, Blossom Budney (Lothrop)

A beginning concept book that may spark young imaginations.

*My Big Golden Counting Book*, Lilian Moore (Golden)

A rhyme by a well-known poet accompanies each clear picture.

*Do Baby Bears Sit on Chairs?*, Ethel and Leonard Kessler (Doubleday)

An old favorite idea book in rhyme.

*Come to the Doctor, Harry*, Mary Chalmers (Harper)

Charming story of Harry Cat, who truthfully represents the fears and triumphs of small children.

*Best Word Book Ever*, Richard Scarry (Golden)

An amazingly comprehensive book, covering many areas of interest in the child's world, with each object carefully labeled. A fine book for youngsters to study alone. Scarry has other appropriate-to-this-age books for eager youngsters.

*The Berenstain Bears First Time Books* (*The Berenstain Bears Visit the Dentist; the Baby Sitter; Moving Day*, etc.), Stan and Jan Berenstain (Random)

Lively tales to allay fears that preschoolers often feel. Inexpensive, comforting, and one step removed from the child himself.

*A B See,* Lucille Ogle and Tina Thoburn (McGraw-Hill)
All about letters and their sounds.

*Green Eyes,* A. Birnbaum (Western)
A young cat's growth to maturity through one year of seasonal changes; greatly appeals to youngsters.

*Happy Winter,* Karen Gundersheimer (Harper)
Children will respond to these many exhilarating winter experiences.

*Yesterday's Snowman,* Gail Mack (Pantheon)
One of the earliest sad feelings must be the realization that snow people melt. A charming small story.

*Go, Dog, Go!,* P. D. Eastman (Random)
Very few words, very zany pictures in cartoon style, make this concept book a long-time favorite.

★*What Do You Say, Dear? A Book of Manners For All Occasions,* Seslye Joslin (Addison-Wesley)
The very zany situations depicted will tickle a youngster's funnybone, yet present him with sound manners.

*Shapes,* John J. Reiss (Bradbury)
Handsome book with fascinating shapes.

*Easy How-To Book,* Seymour Reit (Golden)
Among other basic skills, this great how-to book tells youngsters how to eat spaghetti and open a hard-boiled egg.

*The Little House,* Virginia L. Burton (Houghton Mifflin)
Children empathize with and cheer for the small house slowly surrounded by tall buildings.

*The Snowy Day,* Ezra Jack Keats (Viking, PB)
The simple text and brilliant pictures make vivid a young child's sensory experience of snow.

*A Walk on a Snowy Night,* Judy Delton (Harper)
A charming sensory account of the feel and look of a snowy night.

*Traffic: A Book of Opposites*, Betsy Maestro (Crown)
Bright illustrations highlight the journey of a little car.
★ *More Than One*, Tana Hoban (Macmillan)
Fine photos illustrate the meaning of collective nouns: herd, team, and so forth.
*When We Grow Up*, Anne Rockwell (Dutton)
Detailed, bright pictures of people at work.
*The Animals of Buttercup Farm*, Judy and Phoebe Dunn (Random)
*The Little Duck*, Judy and Phoebe Dunn (Random)
*The Little Rabbit*, Judy and Phoebe Dunn (Random)
These fine books combine simplicity of text and excellence of photography. Just right for preschoolers.
*Trucks*, Gail Gibbons (Crowell)
A good compendium of working trucks that young truck-lovers will pore over.
*Everybody Has a House and Everybody Eats*, Mary McBurney Green (Addison-Wesley)
Beginning perceptions of how these vital needs are met.
*What Do I Say?*, Norma Simon (Albert Whitman)
The social exchanges a young child makes all day (in Spanish and in English).
*Everything Changes*, Morris Philipson (Pantheon)
Another of life's basic truths gently revealed.
*When I Go to the Moon*, Claudia Lewis (Harper, PB)
A child's view of the earth from the moon in poetic prose.
*The Baby Cardinal*, Ellen Galinsky (Putnam)
Fine photographs and a clear text detail the realistic hazards of a baby bird's venturing from its nest.
*ABC of Things*, Helen Oxenbury (Delacorte)
*Numbers of Things*, Helen Oxenbury (Delacorte)
Two charming and rather sophisticated concept books by a fine artist.

*Wordless Books*
After looking through the book with your child, let your child tell you about the book—"read" to you!

*The Snowman*, Raymond Briggs (Random)
   The most beautiful and splendid of the wordless books, this prize-winning book will be cherished by both child and adult.
*Sir Andrew*, Paula Winter (Dial)
   A vain donkey tries to wear too small shoes. Lots of activities in the humorous backgrounds.
*The Good Bird*, Peter Wezel (Harper)
   This enchanting small story about sharing and caring may be hard to find, but worth trying for.
*Changes, Changes*, Pat Hutchins (Macmillan)
   Blocks are formed to make a number of things.
*A Dance For Three*, Ann Schweninger (Dial)
   A charming fantasy to stimulate a child's imagination.
*Do You Want to Be My Friend?*, Eric Carle (Crowell)
   A mouse looks for a companion. The brilliant pictures are somewhat impressionistic.
*Out! Out! Out!*, Martha Alexander (Dial)
   An oldie, but so provocative your child will want to "read" it again and again.
*Lily at the Table*, Linda Heller (Macmillan)
   A child, mouse-size, climbs and plunges into all kinds of delicious goodies.
*A Boy, a Frog, and a Dog*, Mercer Mayer (Scholastic, PB)
   The first of several humorous and wordless frog/boy adventures.
*Deep in the Forest*, Brinton Turkle (Dial)
   A switch on the "Goldilocks" plot with Baby Bear making mischief in a pioneer's cabin.
*The Bear and the Fly*, Paula Winter (Crown)
   Your child will find the fly swatter in each humorous picture.

*Mouse in the House*, Judith Schermer (Houghton Mifflin)
  A family creates havoc trying to oust a mouse.
*Creepy Castle*, John S. Goodall (Atheneum)
  A mouse knight to the rescue! Also his *Surprise Picnic*
  and *The Adventures of Paddy Pork*.

### Poetry for Young Children

Young children respond eagerly, often physically, to vibrant
rhythm and word plays. Try using some of the favorite
poems as an accompaniment to your child's activity, or at
rest time. Be alert to catch your own child's poetic expressions, too.

*Nibble Nibble*, Margaret Wise Brown (Addison-Wesley)
  Wonderful poems to chant over and over. "The Wild
  Black Crows" expresses just the right feelings as you
  and your child see the birds together.
*The Owl and the Pussycat*, Edward Lear (Viking)
  In this fine collection "Jumblies," "runcible spoons,"
  and other wonders may spark your child's own imag-
  inative creativity.
*Everett Anderson's Year*, Lucille Clifton (Holt, Rinehart,
Winston)
  The events in a small boy's year may encourage your
  small child to tell you of some of his doings.
*Any Me I Want to Be*, Karla Kuskin (Harper)
  Fine ideas from a fine poet to open your child's mind
  to new thoughts.
*Poems to Read to the Very Young*, Josette Frank (Random)
  A re-issue of an old favorite, this brightly illustrated
  book has many time-tested poems.
*Up and Down the River: Boat Poems*, Claudia Lewis
(Harper)
  A noted poet's fresh views and images of the river and
  its boats will stimulate young imaginations.
*Every Time I Climb a Tree*, David McCord (Little,
Brown)

*Whispers and Other Poems,* Myra Cohn Livingston (Harcourt Brace)
> A good collection of this popular poet's poems for the young.

*Father Fox's Pennyrhymes,* Clyde Watson (Crowell)
> New verses in a folk-tale format, catchy and fun.

*Catch a Little Rhyme,* Eve Merriam (Atheneum)
> A provocative poet, whose modern style catches children's sensibilities.

*Cecily Parsley's Nursery Rhymes,* Beatrix Potter (Warne)
> From earlier this century, these quaint verses intrigue children today.

*Over in the Meadow,* Ezra Jack Keats (Scholastic, PB)
> A classic poem loved by all children, with great pictures.

*Honey I Love and Other Love Poems,* Eloise Greenfield (Crowell)
> Gentle expression of familial love.

*Under the Green Willow,* Elizabeth Coatsworth (Macmillan)
> A fine poet whose rhythms and rhymes reflect the young child's visions.

### Mother Goose

Fours and fives still love the lively rhythms of Mother Goose verses; now they can chant them, too. And so can you!

*Mother Goose Picture Riddles: A Book of Rebuses,* illustrated by Lisl Weil (Holiday House)
> Fun for those familiar with the old lady's verses.

*One Misty Moisty Morning: Rhymes from Mother Goose,* illustrated by Mitchell Miller (Farrar, Straus, Giroux)
> These less well known but delightful stories give youngsters a fresh look at Old Mother Goose.

*The Mother Goose Book,* illustrated by Alice and Martin Provensen (Random)
> A gorgeously illustrated version of familiar favorites.

*The Mother Goose Treasury,* illustrated by Raymond Briggs (Coward, McCann, Geoghegan)

> A big bright compendium of old favorite tales and verses.

*Old Mother Hubbard,* illustrated by Alice and Martin Provensen (Scholastic, PB)

> Another inexpensive edition, a clear, cosy, and comical depiction of the old lady and her dog.

*Folk Tales*

The old folk tales listed are those whose refrains and plots not only appeal to the very young, but are part of their literary heritage. Fairy stories, with their love themes, are more suitable for older children.

By five, children should know the following stories; you may find other editions and additional folk tales. The more familiar youngsters are with the phrases and themes of these venerable stories, the more they will recognize them in other contexts. In other words, you are not only giving your children a treat, but helping them enlarge their cultural knowledge when you share these folk tales with them.

*The Three Little Kittens,* illustrated by Lorinda Bryan Cauley (Putnam, PB)

> While not strictly a folk tale, this small story has appealed to youngsters through the years.

*The Gingerbread Man,* illustrated by Ed Arno (Scholastic, PB)

*Henny Penny,* illustrated by William Stobbs (Follett, PB)

*The Little Red Hen,* illustrated by Paul Galdone (Scholastic, PB)

*The Three Bears,* illustrated by Paul Galdone (Scholastic, PB)

*The Three Little Pigs,* illustrated by Paul Galdone (Seabury, PB)

*The Old Woman and Her Pig,* illustrated by Paul Galdone (McGraw-Hill)

*The Three Billy Goats Gruff,* illustrated by Marcia Brown (Harcourt Brace Voyager, PB)

*Classics No Child Should Miss*
What is a classic? My own definition is "a book of literary merit that appeals to children over the years"; no doubt you'll have classics of your own to add to this by-no-means comprehensive list. While some of the books on this list may be too old for your child right now, they will be waiting for him later on. Meantime choose those books your child may like—you know your child's tastes best. Most of these books are great for reading aloud.

* *Where the Wild Things Are,* Maurice Sendak (Harper)
     Children identify with Max's wild emotions and his triumph over them. Not for the very young.
*Peter Rabbit,* Beatrix Potter (Frederick Warne)
     This little gem still rivets the attention of pre-schoolers; in the process they are exposed to really fine art. Don't forget Ms. Potter's other small charmers, such as *Jeremy Fisher, Tom Kitten, The Tale of Two Bad Mice, Mrs. Tiggy-Winkle, Squirrel Nutkin,* et al.
*A Child's Garden of Verses,* Robert Louis Stevenson (Puffin, PB)
     Childlike views in verse, still beloved, though some may seem dated.
* *Winnie-the-Pooh,* A. A. Milne (Dutton)
     Pooh and his friends are part of history now; your child may not appreciate them for a year or two, but shouldn't miss hearing them.
*Curious George,* H. A. Rey (Houghton Mifflin)
     George, a small monkey, gets into all kinds of fixes because of his curiosity. Children love this and other books about Curious George because he does all the things they'd like to do themselves!
*Caps for Sale,* Esphyr Slobodkina (Young Scott or Scholastic, PB)

Children love to act out this story of mischievous monkeys teasingly imitating the cap seller.

*The Little Engine that Could*, Watty Piper (Platt & Munk)
An old favorite about a small train that succeeds after trying and trying.

★ *Madeline*, Ludwig Bemelmans (Viking)
The first book of a series of a small activist orphan and her comrades.

★ *The Story of Babar, the Little Elephant*, Jean de Brunhoff (Random)
The first of the Babar books, which will fascinate older youngsters.

★ *The Story of Ping*, Marjorie Flack (Doubleday)
The ever-fascinating story of a small duck on the Yangtse River, full of the charm of another culture and universal childlike feelings.

*Millions of Cats*, Wanda Gag (Coward, McCann, Geoghegan)
An old favorite with an engaging refrain and a satisfactory "ugly duckling" ending.

*The Cat in the Hat*, Dr. Seuss (Random House)
This and other Seuss books often give a child a first fascination with books.

*Blueberries for Sal*, Robert McCloskey (Puffin, PB)
*Make Way for Ducklings*, Robert McCloskey (Puffin, PB)
Children are still captivated by these simple but well-written themes and great pictures.

*Ask Mr. Bear*, Marjorie Flack (Macmillan)
A wonderful birthday present story.

*Nobody Listens to Andrew*, Elizabeth Guilfoile (Scholastic, PB)
Children will understand Andrew's feelings and rejoice with him.

★ *A Bear Called Paddington*, Michael Bond (Dell, PB)
A childhood favorite bear story.

*Gilberto and the Wind*, Marie Hall Ets (Viking)
Small children will know how Gilberto feels as he

experiences all the vagaries of the wind.

★ *Mary Poppins*, P. L. Travers (Harcourt Brace Voyager, PB)

The fantastic events created by this inimitable nanny is really for older kids but may just fascinate your younger child, too. You be the judge.

*Mike Mulligan and His Steam Shovel*, Virginia L. Burton (Houghton Mifflin)

Children identify with the ingenious solution to the dilemma of this helpful steam shovel.

*Sam*, Ann Herbert Scott (McGraw-Hill)

Children empathize with small Sam's feelings of being left out of family activities.

*The Nutshell Library*, Maurice Sendak (Harper)

Four tiny favorite books. Children especially love *Pierre*, who "didn't care," and *Chicken Soup With Rice*.

# CHAPTER
# 7

# *Determining Reading Readiness*

Most schools have some form of assessing the readiness for reading of children entering school. These assessments, called Reading Readiness Tests, are usually made toward the end of kindergarten or at the beginning of grade one; most five- and/or six-year-old children, therefore, will be evaluated as to their capability for starting successfully in a reading program.

These tests vary considerably; the best, but unfortunately far too few, look at the whole child rather than at one part only of her skills. For instance, in some schools, far more than an ability to count or recite the letters of the alphabet is considered. The child meets with the teacher on a one-to-one basis instead of the more usual six-in-a-group testing. The teacher observes the child's fine motor development, how she holds and uses her pencil; her ability to understand sequence, to remember a story, to predict outcomes; her ability to follow directions, using concrete objects, such as, "place the three blocks on the mat; put one block on top of the other"; her reasoning ability and general fund of information.

## GENERAL CONTENT OF TESTS

While there is a great deal of variation from school to school, certain basic skills are common to almost all of them. All reading readiness programs, in one form or another, include the following evaluations:

- understanding and carrying out directions
- seeing similarities and differences
- ability to copy simple designs
- ability to recognize and interpret pictures
- understanding special concepts—*more, less, nearer, farther,* etc.
- understanding word meanings
- hearing and recognizing rhymes
- hearing and comprehending similarities and differences in the initial sound of words
- ability to make sensible judgments on presented facts
- ability to remember the main points of a story and to retell them
- ability to predict outcomes
- ability to name and recognize the letters of the alphabet, and Arabic numerals (our common numbers).

## DON'T START TO PANIC—AND DON'T START TO TEACH

Reading such a list may strike terror into the hearts of some parents. They may yell, "All this stuff sounds too technical! I know my kid doesn't have all this list of abilities—I'd better get cracking and teach him how to cope with this!"

Relax. You *have* been teaching him, every day since he was born. That's what this book is all about—to help raise your consciousness of the importance of the small, daily life opportunities for enhancing your child's skills. It's about the parent's willingness to listen and help to supply materials and relevant experiences, along with the child's freedom to question, explore, and experiment, and draw conclusions.

Look more carefully at the list. Haven't you been encouraging your child to do these very things? Of course, you and your child didn't sit down in a formal way and go over these step by step. Possibly the only formal memorizing your child has done is mentioned in the last-named ability, to know letters and numbers. All the other abilities you have been developing together for some years.

So don't try to start "teaching" these abilities now; your child will pick up on and react to any anxieties you may be harboring—as you know, kids always react to what we wish to hide. And finally, there isn't any one action you can plunge into that will miraculously develop these abilities in your child; they are the result of earlier experiences and learnings.

## REVIEW OF READING READINESS PREPARATIONS

There are, however, many kinds of small activities you can initiate with your child, under the heading of "fun and games." These will, in turn, help strengthen any areas in which you may feel your child is weak. We've suggested a lot of games already just for this kind of development; here are some more that you may want to use, listed under the kind of skill they each may help to develop.

## MOTOR SKILLS AND COORDINATION

The first three are good games for more than one child, but one child can enjoy them, too, especially at those times when a child is housebound.

*Guess What I Am*
The blindfolded child must guess what familiar object is put into her hand by smelling, feeling, listening to it.

*Tightrope Walking*
Lay a line (a rope, tape measure, torn newspaper strips)

across the room and see who can walk on it without "falling off." More than one try is encouraged.

### Feed the Squirrel

Put a pile of nuts or raisins in a dish at one end of the room, at the other end, place a picture of a squirrel, or you can use a bird, elephant, fox, or whatever animal is a child's favorite. The child must carry one nut or raisin from the pile on a book or other flat object across the room to the squirrel. If he does so successfully, he may eat the food.

### Monkey See, Monkey Do

This game consists of physically imitating the "leader" who may jump, run, skip, hop, crawl, etc.

## UNDERSTANDING AND MAKING JUDGMENTS

A basically important ongoing task is to develop comprehension and extend your child's knowledge by asking questions that require her to predict outcomes, to make comparisons, to see relationships, to make judgments. Some specific suggestions are:

- presenting an assortment of pictures that show different categories such as: household objects and cars, fruits and animals, flags and boats, and so on. Encourage child to rearrange those things that "go together"; she may paste them on paper, cut them out, or just pile them up.
- looking together at pictures, or wordless story books, and asking your child to tell you what's happening. Ask judgmental questions, such as, "Why do you think he did that?" "How do you think she feels?" "What do you think happened after?"
- playing games that require a child to differentiate between left and right, up and down, behind and before, on top of and underneath. This can be done casually as well, in everyday tasks, for instance: "Please put a fork on the left side of each plate and a knife on the right side

of each plate." "Put your books on top of the table and your boots under the table." "Please stand behind me" (in front of me, beside me). "Raise your right hand, put your left foot in front of you." Group games, such as "I put my left foot in, I put my left foot out, I give my hands a clap, clap, clap, and turn myself about," are fun, too, and help the child distinguish between left and right. using everyday opportunities to help the child observe consequences, causes and results, predict outcomes, as in the following examples:

"Look, it's raining. Where does the rain come from? Do you know where it goes? Will it make a hole in the roof? Does it hurt to walk in the rain? What happens to you when you go out in the rain? When the sun comes out, what happens to the puddles?" (Of course, you don't sling all these questions at your child in one volley, but use one or two when the occasion presents itself.)

"What does jelly taste like? peanut butter? spaghetti? What is squishy?" (Start off, if the child seems hesitant. Volunteer what seems squishy to you.) "What is cold? hot? What tickles? How does sunshine feel? What does clay feel like? What do you like to do in the rain? What hurts?" These are just suggestions to help you see the many ways in which you can enrich your child's sensory perceptions and recall of sensory experiences.

You may use a walk together to help the child predict possible outcomes. "If the red car on that street doesn't stop at the corner, what do you think would happen? If that child leans too far out of the window, what may happen? That dog is begging for something the boy is holding; what is he begging for? Yes, ice cream. If the dog keeps jumping on the boy, what might happen? Uh-oh, if nobody fixes that hanging board, what will happen?"

## MEMORY AND RECALL OF DETAILS; VOCABULARY DEVELOPMENT

All through this book, emphasis has been placed on engaging the child in verbal communication, in listening to stories and verses, in asking questions about the material read aloud, in eliciting comments on all manner of things, even in the production of her own stories. The best and most rewarding technique is to continue in the same way.

Perhaps you might want to read more to your child, to encourage your child to share the reading by repeating the refrains, or other obvious words. And surely this is the time to increase the amount of "writing" your child does.

Some of this "writing" may actually be the child's own attempts to spell his name, to copy the title of his book or paper. Most of it will be *your* writing, the taking down of his stories or informational accounts of experiences, of his thoughts, his conclusions—but gaily illustrated by his art work.

Five-year-old Scott Jelwyn's mother "wrote up" his excited account of a butterfly's emergence from a cocoon. Scott listened with satisfaction to his story, illustrated it plentifully, and later asked his mother to read it over several times. Finally, Scott himself was able to recite proudly the two pages. Some of the recitation was just memorizing, some was actual recognition of words; but this kind of experience provides a solid basis for the skills necessary in independent reading later.

"Butterfly"
by Scott Jelwyn
We found a cocoon, a tight little cocoon.
It looked like a teeny lunch bag.
We put it in the jar with some sticks. And leaves.
Mommy put holes in the top of the jar for breath.
In a morning, a big butterfly was there!
Swinging and swinging its wings.
An orange and black butterfly.
And the cocoon was all squashed empty!

# PRACTICES AND PROBLEMS IN READINESS TESTING

Most children have not been accustomed to the kinds of tests given for reading readiness. While the child may well be cognizant of the answers, he may be tripped up by the format or physical requirements of the test, such as identifying the correct row, the kind of marking required, the kind of answer desired. Other very important aspects of school testing that may interfere with desired results are:

· unfamiliarity with the setting
· unfamiliarity with the teacher
· unfamiliarity with the other children
· physical illness or sleepiness or mental distraction or shyness
· lack of desire to do the activity at that time.

These and other less tangible causes may result in inaccurate indications of the child's true abilities and skills.

Of course, most school testers are also aware of these difficulties and make allowances for them, such as not giving the tests until the children are well acquainted with the tester, or not giving a child a test when the teacher feels he is not up to par.

Sometimes slip-ups do occur, however; thus some prior experience with the format or makeup of the type of testing given in schools can be of great help to your child.

## Practicing for Testing

There are a number of practice sheets presented here, so that you and your child may become accustomed to the kind of experience he will probably face in school. But before using the practice sheets with your child, here are some important cautions:

· DON'T use these as tests, but as games to play.
· DON'T use them for "grading" your child, but to highlight areas that need strengthening.
· DO read them over carefully at first, both the instruc-

tions and the practice sheets, so that you will sound and act naturally when presenting the material to the child.
· DO stop if your child seems anxious or bored.

*Things to Remember*
There is no score, no right or wrong to mark—just a chance to find out where your child needs specific help.

A relaxed, eager approach to a testing situation is one of the *most important* factors for success. Unfortunately, some children become frightened by the way tests are administered, and thus don't live up to their real capabilities.

These practice sheets should help your child view such exercises as enjoyable. If, by even an inner concern for your child's success, you begin to press your child, the result will not only be unsatisfactory, but may set up an apprehensive attitude on the child's part that will carry over negatively to such future exercises. If you yourself view these practice sheets as "tests" of your child's abilities, you are already creating a "win-fail" atmosphere.

Please think of these games as:
· an opportunity for your child to use the kind of material and directions that, in one form or another, he will experience on entering school
· an opportunity for you to observe some of your child's skills and knowledge
· a chance for you to begin to fill in the gaps and lacks you perceive in such knowledge, provided that you do so in an informal way, a "play" way, that fits easily into your child's daily routine.

## DIRECTIONS FOR USING PRACTICE SHEEETS

1. Read the material beforehand and look carefully at what the child is requested to do, so that you will talk naturally. Use your own words if you like, once you understand the directions and aim of the sheet. Use the practice sheets in the order presented.

2. If your child doesn't seem to understand a direction or hesitates at an answer, HELP HIM. This is not a test, but a practice sheet.

3. At the same time, note the areas where your child seems weakest. It might be in seeing differences, or judging outcomes. Don't write down any observations—that might make the child anxious.

4. If you have observed areas where the child's knowledge and/or skills need strengthening, use the practice sheet as a guide for making your own sheets in the desired area.

5. Ask your child's help in drawing the pictures or thinking of ideas. The more the child is involved in creating the tests, the better he will learn them. HAVE FUN!

6. These practice sheets give the child a chance to become familiar with the most commonly used testing techniques, such as indicating a choice by drawing a diagonal line through it, underlining, filling in a circle, or drawing a ring around what the child thinks is a correct answer.

## PRACTICE SHEETS

*1. Visual Discrimination: Matching Shapes*
Show your child the practice sheet and say: "This is a seeing-and-marking game. The page is filled with rows of different shapes, isn't it? In front of each row is a little object all by itself.

"Look at the top of the page. In front of the first row is a funny-shaped line, like a curving road. Put your finger on it. Now move your finger to the next picture in that row. Is it the same shape as the curving-road shape? Yes, it is. Draw a line across it from corner to corner. [Help your child draw a line from the lower left corner across to the upper right corner. It doesn't have to be very straight.] Look at the rest of the pictures in that row. Do any more pictures match the curving-road shape? Draw a line on each one you find. Yes, there are *two* pictures that match the same curving-road shape as the first one.

"Now look at the next row. Put your finger on the picture all by itself at the beginning. What kind of shape is it? [If child says it is a "snail shape," use that term. However the child identifies it (curly-around, hop-scotch game, etc.) use that word. In the same way, use whatever word the child uses for succeeding rows.]

"Yes, it looks like a . . . snail shape. Now move your finger across that row, look carefully at each picture. Then draw a line across each picture with the exact same snail shape as the picture one.

"Now look at the third row. What is the first shape called? Yes, a triangle. Put your finger under each picture in that row and look carefully. Are there any more pictures of triangles? Watch out! There's a tricky one here. One of the triangles may be upside down, but it is still a triangle."

If your child objects to saying picture 4 is exactly like the first one, agree with him; he's being very meticulous and just as correct as the child who does mark number 4 as being like the original triangle.

Help your child identify shapes at the beginning of the next four rows, and ask her to draw a line on those that are the same shape in that row.

*Remember:* This is a *game,* not a *test.*

Don't let your child work at it more than twenty minutes.

If your child wants to do more, have *her* draw a page of pictures and choose the shapes *you* are to identify.

## 2. Auditory/Visual Discrimination: Matching Initial Sounds

Show your child the practice sheet and say: "This is another kind of listening and writing game. The puzzle this time is to find the pictures that start with the same sound. Listen: *bear ball bike barn* all start with the same sound, don't they? What sound do they start with? *Buh,* that's right. [If your child doesn't say the sound, you say it for her. If she calls it the B sound, tell her that's right, but add that the B sound is *buh*.]

"Look at the row of pictures at the top of the page. In front of that first row is a ball, all by itself. Put your finger on it.

1. *Visual Discrimination* MATCHING SHAPES

## 2.   *Auditory/Visual Discrimination* MATCHING INITIAL SOUNDS

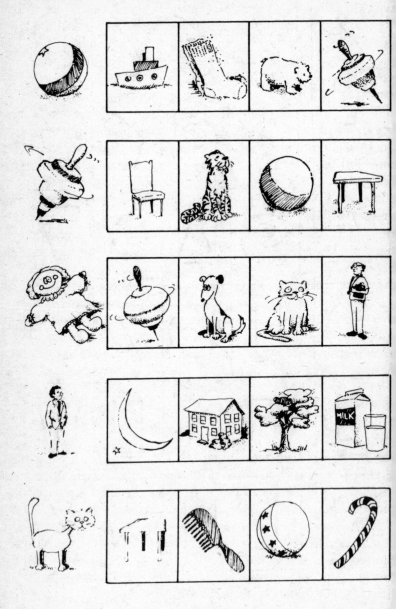

Good. Now move your finger across to the first picture in that row: what is that a picture of? Yes, a *boat*. Does *boat* start with the same sound as the *ball* at the beginning of the row? Yes, it does. So draw a line across the picture of the *boat*. Put your finger under each picture in that row. Do any of those pictures start with the *buh* sound? Yes, the *bear* does. Now you found two pictures, *boat* and *bear*, that start with the same sound. Draw a line through the bear also.

"Now look at row 2. What is the picture all by itself at the beginning of the row? Yes, a *top*, a spinning *top*. What sound does *top* begin with? Yes, the *tuh* sound. Find the other pictures in that row that begin with the tuh sound and draw a line on them. Can you make the same line from one corner to another that you made in the first game? [Help your child to draw a slanting line catty-corner from lower left to upper right.] Good. You marked the *tiger* and *table*. What sound do *tiger* and *table* begin with? Yes, the tuh sound, just like the beginning of *top*. So you draw a line across it. What pictures did you mark? Yes, the *tiger* and *table*. Good for you!

"Now the game gets harder. We'll both say the name of the picture in front of each row. Listen carefully for the sound that the picture begins with. Then you go ahead across each row and put a line on all the pictures in the row that begin with the same sound."

Help your child say the key word at the beginning of the row. Give her plenty of time to identify and mark similar beginning sounds in each row. Help her draw the line if she asks.

*Remember:* This is a *game,* not a *test.*

Don't let your child work at it more than twenty minutes.

If your child wants to do more, have *her* draw a page of pictures and choose the sounds *you* are to identify.

### 3. *Auditory/Visual Discrimination: Number Concepts*

Show your child the practice sheet and say: "This game has lots of things for you to do. Look carefully at the pictures and listen carefully before you mark the answers.

"Look at the top of the page. There is a row of pictures, each in a little box. Some of the boxes have more than one thing in them. In front of the top row is the number 1. Number 1 is in front of row 1. Put your finger on the number 1. There are balloons in each box after the 1. Find the box with one balloon in it, and draw a line across the one balloon. [Help your child if needed. Show him how to draw a line— no matter how crooked—from the lower left corner of the box to the top right corner.] Fine!

"Now look at row 2. Row 2 is under row 1; it has a 2 at the beginning of the row. There is a number in each box after the 2. Can you find the box with a 2 in it? Fine! [Remember, help if it's needed.] Draw a line across the box with the number 2 in it.

"Can you find row 3? Row 3 is under row 2. Row 3 has the number 3 in front of it, at the beginning of row 3. Put your finger on row 3. Now look at the pictures in the boxes in row 3. Each picture has children in it. Next to each group of children is the number that says how many children are in that box. Look at the first box after number 3. There are how many children in that box? Two; yes, two children. Put your finger on the number 2 in that box. Right.

"Now look at the rest of the boxes in row 3. Can you find the box that has three children in it, and the number 3 written in it? Draw a line across the box with three children. [As usual, help if needed.]

"Now look at row 4 at the bottom of the page. Row 4 has the number 4 in front of it. Put your finger on the number 4. Look at the cats in the boxes in row 4. Can you see the box with a group of four cats in it? Put your finger on the box with four cats in it. Good for you!

"This time, you are going to do something a little different. You are going to write the number 4 in the box with four cats in it! Use the space above the cats—it doesn't matter if you write over the lines or on the cats too!"

Help the child if needed. Don't let him feel he must fit the

3. *Auditory/Visual Discrimination* NUMBER CONCEPTS

number into the space, but he can feel free to write it as large as he likes.

·*Remember:* This is a *game*, not a *test*.

Don't let your child work at it more than twenty minutes.

If your child wants to do more, you draw a page of numbers and let him be the teacher for at least half the numbers, while you mark the numbers he names.

### 4. *Auditory/Visual Discrimination: Identifying Objects*

Show your child the practice sheet and say: "This is a listening game. Look at the rows of small pictures on this page. We'll say the pictures' names together, then you'll find one picture when I name it.

"Look at the row—the line-up—of pictures at the very top of the page. In front of the top row there's a picture of a leaf. Can you find it? Good. Put your finger on it. [Help your child, if necessary, whenever he seems puzzled, by helping him move his finger to the correct picture.]

"Now move your finger across the page, pointing to each picture as we name the thing or things in that picture. Okay?

"The first picture is a ball, the second picture is a boat, the third picture is a car, and the fourth picture is a doll. Now find the picture of the *car* and draw a line under it, like this. [Help the child draw a line under the picture. Accept any wavy or crooked mark; this is not a drawing practice.]

"Look at the second row, the row with the star in front of it. Let's say the names of the pictures in the *star* row: house, tree, sun, moon. Good, you have named all of them.

"Now find the picture of the *tree* and draw the same kind of line under it."

In the same way, continue with the next two rows. Help your child place his finger on the identifying mark at the beginning of each row. Help him move his finger from left to right across the page, naming the objects aloud with you. Have him find the picture you choose in rows 3 and 4; and

## 4. *Auditory/Visual Discrimination* IDENTIFYING OBJECTS

help him, if necessary, to draw the line left to right under the picture you name.

The last row, row 5, has two objects in each picture. Follow the above instructions for that row, too.

*Remember:* This is a *game,* not a *test.*

Don't let your child work at it more than twenty minutes.

If your child wants to do more, *you* draw a page of pictures and let *him* be the teacher for at least half the pictures, while you mark the pictures he names.

### 5. *Visual Discrimination: Recognizing Likeness and Difference*

Show your child the practice sheet and say: "What's the difference between a dog and a cat, anyhow? They're both furry pets, they both have ears, tails, and four legs. What's different about them? [Accept any answer. If answer is only true in child's personal experience, such as a dog's ears hang down and a cat's ears stand up, accept and add to it.] Okay, some dogs' ears hang down and some dogs' ears stand up, but *all* cats' ears stand up, don't they?

"We're going to try to find things that are exactly the same, that aren't different at all. Look at the top row of pictures on this page. There's a big A in front of the top row. Put your finger on the A. Good. Now look at the boxes after the A. Each box has two faces in it, right. Some have different expressions on them, like crying, or frowning, or talking, or smiling. Can you find the box where two faces have the same expression? The box with two faces that look exactly alike?

"Great! Now draw a line under the box with the look-alike faces in it."

[As before, help your child to find the answer if she seems hesitant. Ask her—and help her—to name the various expressions, then to spot the look-alikes. Help her to underline, if needed; the kind of line she makes—crooked, wavering—doesn't matter at all. It takes lots of practice to draw straight lines.]

"Look at the row under row A. This row has a big B in

5. *Visual Discrimination* RECOGNIZING LIKENESS AND
DIFFERENCE

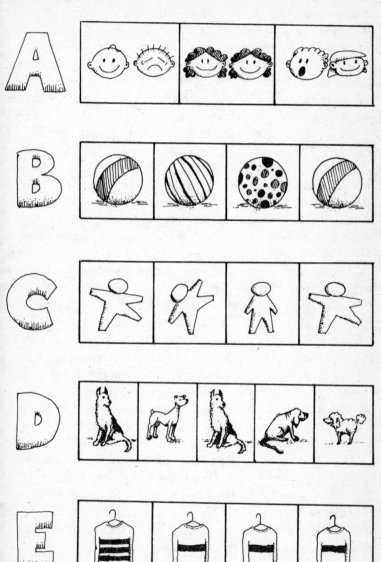

front of it. Can you put your finger on the B? Now look at the pictures of all the balls in that row. Can you find and underline—draw a line under—the balls that are exactly alike, that look just like each other?" (As in row A, give help if needed. Accept any kind of line.)

In the same way, guide your child through rows C and D. After guiding child to row E, say, "Now we'll do something different. This time, we'll look for the shirt that is *different,* that's not the same as the other three shirts. Good, you found it! Now draw a line under the shirt that's different." [As always, help the child if needed.]

Follow-up activity: Try to create another page of likes-unlikes with your child helping, either directing or drawing.

### 6. Visual Discrimination: Classifying and Categorizing
Show your child the practice sheet and say: "Here are pictures of four things in each row. Three pictures are pictures of things that go together; one picture does *not* go together with the other three—does not *belong* with the others.

"Look at the top of the page. Put your finger on the number 1. That is for row 1. Look at the pictures in row 1 and tell me what they are. Yes, a teddy bear, some blocks, a toy train, and some apples. Which three things go together? Yes, the teddy bear, the blocks, and the toy train: these are all things children play with. Apples are for eating—they don't belong with play things, do they? Draw a line across the picture of the apples, because they don't belong to the others; they don't go with the others."

Help your child to name the objects, to see the relationships; this may be a new way for her of looking at things. Do the rest of the page in the same way; give your child all the help she needs. This is PRACTICE, not a TEST. Ask your child to make up her own series to test out on you. The teacher usually learns as much as the student.

### 7. Visual Discrimination: Letter Recognition
Show your child the practice sheet and say: "Here is another

6. *Visual Discrimination* CLASSIFYING AND CATEGORIZING

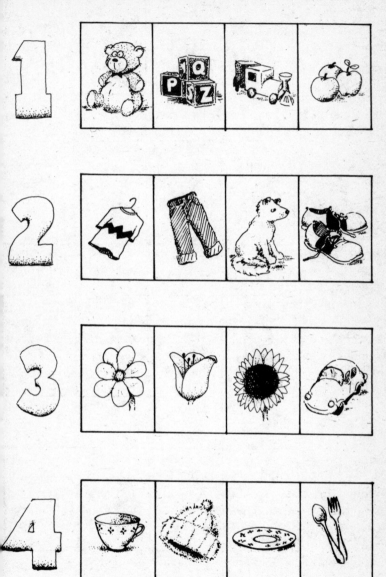

interesting game, a letter game, for us to play. We are going to mark this paper differently, too. Look at the top of your page: there is a row of letters, each in a little frame or box. In front of the top row is the number 1. Can you put your finger on the number 1? [Help child if needed. Your child shouldn't feel pressured or nervous about finding the correct row or making a mark. If your child seems worried, suggest putting the game away for another time.] Good!

"There are three letters in the row of boxes after the 1. Do you know them? Can you tell me their names? Good!

"Under each letter is a little circle. Will you show it to me? Fine! Put your finger on the A. Right! Now you are going to fill in the little circle under the A with your pencil. Fill it all in, so no white paper shows. [At first, your child may be very sloppy at this not-so-easy job. It's hard to fill a tiny circle without slopping over. Accept the child's work without any negative comment or attempts to help. He'll be okay as his muscular coordination develops.]

"Now look at row 2. It's right under row 1, and has a 2 in front of the boxes. Can you tell me the names of the letters in that row, row 2? Good for you! Now fill in the circle under the T, the T circle, please, just as you did before."

Continue the same way with Row 3. At row 4, say: "Here's a row with two letters in each box. Row 4 has two letters in each box. Can you put your finger on the number 4 in front of row 4? Good. Now read the letters in the first box. S T, that's right. Read the letters in the other boxes; good. Can you fill in the circle under G E, the circle under the letters G E?"

For the last line, row 5, say: "Look at the last line, the bottom line. The number 5 is in front of that bottom line. Put your finger on the number 5 in front of row 5. Now look at the letters in the boxes in Row 5. Do they look different from the letters in the boxes above row 5? Yes, they do. These are the little letters, not the big letters. Can you read them?"

Your child may not be as familiar with these "manuscript"

or lower-case letters as he is with the capital or upper-case letters above. If he hesitates, read them aloud yourself as you point to each. You may suggest that the child fill in a circle under a letter you choose, if he seems comfortable enough with the lettering. Otherwise, skip it. Or, suggest that *you* fill in the circle and your child choose the letter.

*Remember:* This is a *game,* not a *test.*

Don't let your child work at it more than twenty minutes.

If your child wants to do more, you draw a page of letters and let him be the teacher for at least half the letters, while you mark the letters he names.

### 8. Auditory Discrimination: Hearing Directions

Show your child the practice sheet and say: "This is a listening game. Look at this page full of little pictures. The little pictures are in rows, or lines. Each picture has a small circle under it. There is a little picture all by itself in front of each row.

"Look at the top of the page. Do you see a little heart at the front of the row? Put your finger on the little heart. [Help your child if he seems puzzled.] Now let's look at the row of pictures after the heart. There are two things in each picture. Let's say their names together: boy/man; woman/girl; man/man.

"Now close your eyes and listen. I'm going to name one of the pictures—don't peek! Woman/girl. Now open your eyes and point to that picture. Good for you! Let's mark that picture by filling in the little circle under it. Color in the little circle under "woman/girl" with your pencil. Good!

"Now look at the next row of pictures, the one with a little flower in front of it. Put your finger on each picture as we name it, okay? Mouse/cat; cat/cat; cat/dog. Shut your eyes again and listen. Cat/dog. Open your eyes, find the picture I said, and fill in the little circle under it. Good!

"Let's make the game a little harder. This time we won't first say the name out loud. Look at the row with the flag in front of it. Put your finger on the flag. Close your eyes and

7. *Visual Discrimination* LETTER RECOGNITION

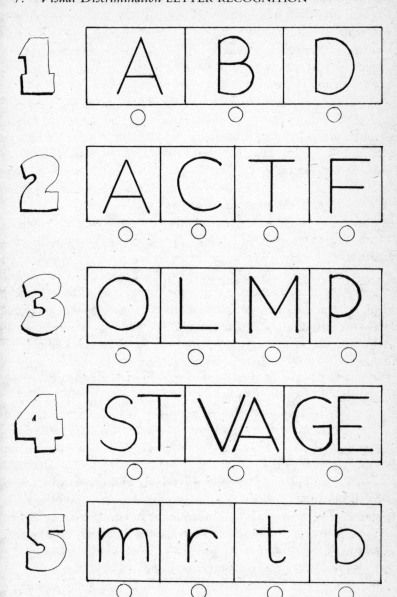

listen. Remember, don't peek. Horse/house. Now open your eyes, find the picture I named, and fill in the circle under it. Great!"

In the same way, do lines three and four. You pick out the picture you want your child to choose. Have your child fill in the correct circle.

*Remember:* Don't make this a *test,* but a *game.*

If your child wants to go on, have *him* make some pictures, and *you* do the guessing!

Don't, in any case, let your child work at this more than twenty minutes.

### 9. Auditory Discrimination: Rhyming

Show your child the practice sheet and say: "Here's a rhyming game: words that sound alike, even if they start with different letters—like *moon, spoon, tune.*

"Look at the rows of pictures on this page. In front of each row there's a number. Look at the top row of pictures—the pictures at the top of the page. Put your finger on the number in front of that row, the number 1. [Help your child to do so, also to finger each picture in row 1 as you both name the objects in each picture.]

"Let's say the names of the things in each picture after the number 1, okay?

"Car, hat, balloon, bike. Now listen to the word I say: Cat. Look at the pictures in row 1 again. Which one rhymes with *cat,* sounds like *cat.* Does *cat* rhyme with *car?* with *hat?*"

If your child doesn't say yes, continue with rest of row. Then ask your child to say each picture and the word *cat.* If your child still doesn't get correct rhyme, don't go on with game. Assure your child that he or she has done well, but has done enough for today. Then help the child recognize rhymes in a leisurely way, by reading poetry, Mother Goose; by rhyming words yourself when opportunity arises, when nonsense rhymes can be used, i.e., "Do you eat your *cake* with a *rake?*" "Can you eat the *moon* with a *spoon?*" "I love you as high as a *tree,* as deep as the *sea.*"

8. *Auditory Discrimination* HEARING DIRECTIONS

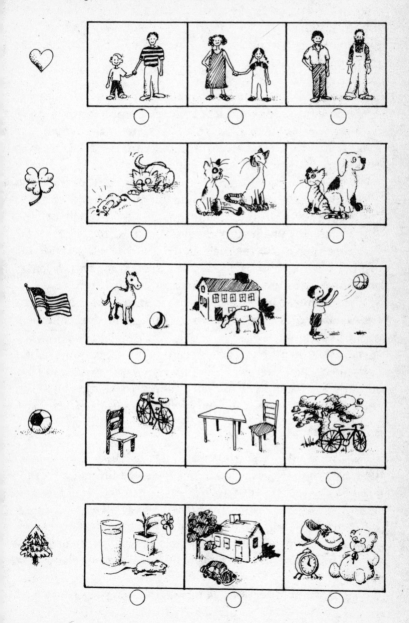

If your child catches the right rhyme, however, finish the page in the same way. Help the child to fill in the circle under the picture that rhymes with the word you say. The word in the following parentheses (at the end of each row) is the rhyming word you say.

*10. Making Judgments and Comparisons: Recalling Information*
The best education is not just collecting a dry store of information; it is *using* that store of facts to make your own judgments, to see relationships, to create new ideas—and always to enlarge your knowledge.

Such a way of thinking begins in childhood: the child who is encouraged to question, to imagine possibilities, to think creatively, to enlarge her fund of knowledge, will be best able to face the challenges of school, and of life.

Opportunities for helping your child develop these capabilities are around every day; it just requires an awareness on your part to use daily events as subject matter.

The following practice sheets are examples of the kinds of critical awareness we want to encourage in our children's way of thinking.

But don't overdo it. The aim is to try to slip in judgmental questions when they seem appropriate, not to overwhelm our kids with them. Letting our children ask us the same kind of questions helps also, not only in keeping us in the learner's role too, but also in boosting the children's morale as they become the teacher.

As always, don't be concerned if your child doesn't give the answer you expect: children's ways of thinking are quite unique. Ask, however, if your child can tell you why he chose that answer. His reasons may be excellent.

Again, this is not a true/false quiz but just another way of encouraging your child to see relationships, predict outcomes, and make his own judgments—an ongoing daily process.

Use the same directions as in previous games. Your child will fill in the circles under the answers.

## 9. *Auditory Discrimination* RHYMING

Show your child the pictures and say:

1. "The boy can't open the door, because he has forgotten something. Which of these three things has he forgotten? Fill in the circle under the thing the boy has forgotten."

2. "John says, 'Here are some animals that usually are not pet animals. Yet two of them sometimes live in people's houses.' Color in the circles under the two animals that sometimes live in people's houses."

3. "Judy sees four animals in the park. She sees a dog, a grasshopper, a squirrel, and a bluejay. 'Come here!' Judy calls. One animal comes to Judy, the other three animals go away. Fill in the circle under the animal that comes to Judy."

4. "David is going to visit a farm. 'Oh, boy!' David says. 'I love to look at farm animals.' Fill in the circle under the animals that David may see at the farm."

5. "Sandy, Curly, and Spot are three dogs. Sandy is bigger than Curly. Curly is bigger than Spot. Fill in the circle under Spot."

6. "Roberto spilled a glass of water on the kitchen floor. Fill in the circle under the picture that shows what Roberto did next."

*11. Making Judgments and Recalling Information; Noting Details; Spatial Concepts*

Show your child the practice sheet and say: "This game is different from the other games, and we're going to make a new mark. We're going to draw a ring around the answer. Here's how we do it.

"I'm going to ask you a question. You look at the pictures, then tell me the answer. You can draw a ring around your answer, too. Okay? Let's look at the two pictures at the top on the left side, the two pictures right after the big letter A. Here is the question. [Read it to the child.] Point to the right answer, and tell it to me. Yes, the broom. Can you make a ring around the broom? Good for you."

11.   *Making Judgments, Recalling Information* GENERAL
KNOWLEDGE, NOTING DETAILS, SPATIAL CONCEPTS

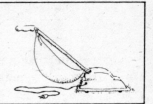

Which is the broom?

Which makes more noise?

Which cat is *under* the tree?

Which airplane (jet) is *over the water?*

Which one is the fire hydrant?

Which flag is *on top of* the castle?

Which dog is *behind* the horse?

Which pumpkin has a *mad* face?

As before, help the child make the ring. It doesn't have to be neat or go around the whole object. In the same way, do questions B through H with your child in alphabetical order.

## 11A.　*Making Judgments, Recalling Information* GENERAL KNOWLEDGE, NOTING DETAILS, SPATIAL CONCEPTS

The two animals here are drawn the same size.
In real life, which animal is bigger?

Which child is farthest from the barn?

Which animal is a wild animal?

Which child is *nearer* to the balloon man?

Which animal has *four* legs?

Which cat is the *youngest?*

Which chair is the *widest?*

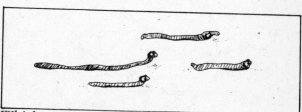

Which worm is the *longest?*

For further practice have your child answer questions 1–8 on practice sheet 11-A.

*12. Finishing a Story: Making Judgments; Predicting Outcomes*
A. (Use the same directions as in practice sheet 11 for making a ring around the answer your child chooses. Then ask the child to focus attention on row A.) "Here are three pictures: a picture of a boy and girl jumping rope, a picture of a boy and girl eating hot dogs, and a picture of a boy and girl in the water. I'm going to tell you a story; you listen and then you can finish the story.

> Linda and Stephen were very hot. "Let's get cool," said Linda.
> "Yes, let's cool off," Stephen answered.
> What did Linda and Stephen do to cool off?

"Now, look at the three pictures. Draw a ring around the picture that shows how Linda and Stephen cooled off."

Help your child make the ring if he seems hesitant, or do it for him at first if he wants you to. As his confidence grows, he will be willing to try doing it himself.

In the same way, read the other four stories and ask him to draw a ring around the picture that shows how the story ends. If you are puzzled by his choice, ask him to explain—but accept whatever he says. The important aim here is for him to *enjoy* the game.

Little Bear looked out of the cave. Snow was falling fast. A cold wind was blowing.

"Brrr!" said Little Bear. "I will have to stay warm."

"Show what Little Bear did to stay warm. Draw a ring around the picture that shows what Little Bear did."

Mary Ann looked at her bike. Something was missing from her bike. Something to put her things in.

"I can't ride my bike like this. But I know how to fix it," she said. "Then I can ride it again." She ran off to get the missing thing.

"Draw a ring around Mary Ann putting the missing thing on her bike."

Jake said, "My throat feels very dry, as dry as dust. I must do something to help my throat feel less dry.

"Draw a ring around the picture that shows Jake doing something to help his throat."

Lynn's uncle gave her an aquarium. It was a big glass tank filled with water. It also had a little stone island in it with a plant growing on it.

Her uncle said, "You may choose two animals to live in the tank aquarium. They must be animals who always live in the water, or animals who live in the water but sometimes like to climb on the rock!"

"Which two animals did Lynn choose?"

# CHAPTER
# 8

# *The Beginning of School—and After*

At last, the big day is here. No matter if your child has been to a day-care group or to nursery school, these are preschools; this is the beginning of what she calls "real school." It is also her first big step toward independence; she will be acting on her own each day without your guiding help.

Most parents have mixed feelings when that first day comes. They are proud of and excited for their child; they hope they have done enough to prepare her for this new adventure; and they are uncertain of their role now. How will the school teach their child to read? Will they, the parents, be allowed to help at home? Or will they be told, "hands off"?

## THE FIRST STEP

One of the most important steps you can take is to get to know your child's teacher, the school principal, and their educational program, well ahead of the first day of school. Probably the best time to set up an appointment with your child's teacher and/or principal is at least by the spring before your child goes to school. If you can visit a class earlier, that's great. There's nothing like seeing an educational theory in action to help you understand it.

Naturally, your first questions will be about your child entering (or not entering) school in the fall. You will want to find out how the school:

· determines the entering age either for kindergarten or first grade
· determines when a child is ready to begin formal reading.

### Determining the Entering Age

Many schools have a structured method of school entrance. One school may accept in kindergarten any child who will be five by December 1. Thus, the September kindergarten may contain children who were five the previous January, and are now five years and seven months, as well as children who are only four years and nine months old—a very wide gap in ages and perhaps in capabilities. Your job is to find out what entering time would be best for *your* child. Hopefully the school will help you make important decisions, such as, should your four-year-old wait a year so he won't be the youngest child in class? The same strictures may apply also for entrance to first grade.

### Determining the Beginning Reading Age

In the past, formal teaching of reading was reserved for the first grade; kindergarten promoted "reading readiness" skills. Many schools today, however, begin such formal teaching in kindergarten, perhaps because of pressures from our adult "hurry-up" world—which may or may not be to the child's advantage.

We know that success in formal reading occurs when a child is fully ready, mentally, emotionally, and physically, for this important job. Thus, we have the right—and the necessity—of finding out how the school determines when the child has reached this stage of being ready to read. Does the school have a formal reading program, beginning at a certain date, say, the second month of the first year? Or does the school have a freer program, which allows children to begin reading when they show a desire to do so, no matter whether they are in kindergarten or first grade?

Does the school test the child for reading readiness? If so, what kinds of tests are given? Or does the school determine readiness to read by some other means, such as the child's mental or actual age? (The child's mental age is also determined by testing.)

Perhaps no tests at all are given, and the child is presumed ready to read when the teacher says he is, or just because he is in first grade.

Many parents have found it helps to use the kinds of practice sheets suggested in chapter 7 in order to have some objective estimate of their child's readiness to read. Other parents have used the sheets not only for their own satisfaction, but to share with the school.

## MAKING A BRIDGE BETWEEN HOME AND SCHOOL

Making a bridge between home and school is of the utmost importance. Your sense of personal concern and friendly interest in the school will help the teacher to respond in an equally friendly way. Some of us, however, are reluctant to visit school; perhaps our own childhood experiences make us dread the smell of chalk and wet rubber boots, or the sound of feet running in the echoing halls. For such parents—and all others who prefer a more intimate surrounding than the classroom—a good first step would be to invite your child's future teacher to lunch. If she can come to your house, fine. She and your child can meet and talk together for a short while. But be sure to arrange for your child to leave then— perhaps to a friend's house for lunch, or even to play in his own room—so that he won't overhear your discussion. It's better to talk about a child in his absence, so he won't misunderstand or be upset.

Whether you meet in school or at home, ask about the school's reading method, and how you can help. The teacher may give you specific or more generalized advice; you might share with her what you have been doing to prepare your child for reading. Chances are, whether or not she gives you directions for working with your child at home, she will welcome the kind of "reading readiness" you've been doing, and urge you to continue it. The kind of preparation proposed in this book can only enhance and enlarge any school program.

This is a solid first step in building that bridge of friendly relationship between home and school, which will become firmer as the years pass. Your interest, your willingness to help out, your support of the personnel and teachings of the school can only strengthen the developing relationship between your child and his school.

In the course of time you may disagree with some of the school's methods and/or teachers. Your child may complain that "Mr. Garney isn't as nice as Mrs. Lothrop. He yells when we act silly. He's mean!"

You have to keep as broad a view as possible; unless a teacher is really incompetent, children learn to accustom themselves to new ways. And in the process, they also learn that people act differently, that one can't always have what one desires, but must accommodate to change—wonderful and practical knowledge that will help your child in all aspects of life.

## The Helping Parent Still Helps

But this doesn't mean you leave your child to face a difficult situation alone. You continue to help her at home; most of the time, your help is generalized, as it was in preschool days. Only on occasion do you offer specific help; for instance, in learning spelling words, you can serve as an audience for your child. Or you can reinforce her knowledge of short vowel sounds by helping her find them in books, signs, or newspapers. At rare times, you may even help your child to read or do math—but not unless you judge the child's need can only be met by such direct assistance. On the whole, your help will be of the "enlarging" kind where you are:

- reinforcing the concepts your child learns at school
- stretching your child's imagination in broadening the concepts she learns
- providing as many concrete examples as possible to make your child's work more vivid and lifelike.

## Reinforcing Concepts

One of the best ways to reinforce the concepts learned at school is to continue the kind of games you have been playing with your child even before she went to school. Take "Alphabet Cards" (described on page 165), for instance: now you can play a more advanced game by printing on the cards words your child is learning; vowel and consonant sounds presented in school with appropriate pictures for each: A is

for *a*pple 🍎    B is for *b*all 🏀    and so on. Or you can

match word families, such as the *AT* group, with explanatory pictures, like *C*at, *B*at, *R*at.

C 🐱        B 🏏        R 🐭

Such concrete games are not the only way to reinforce concepts for reading success. On the street, in the stores, around the house are rich sources for informal learning. For instance, while shopping, you might say to your child, "Can you bring me a loaf of something that begins with B, *buh?* Get our favorite kind with the Big A and daisies printed on it."

Or, when walking home, you might say, "When we get to the corner, I want to go on Park Street. Can you find it for me? Let's look at the street signs and see which sign begins with P, *puh.*" But don't belabor these activities. Keep them light and simple.

After school each day it's important that your child get plenty of rest, relaxation, and lots of time for both physical exercise and dramatic play. However, very often the first grader wants some "homework" to do, like the older children. If you can reinforce some of her new skills in a simple playful way, you can be sure you are really helping, not hurting. One of the saddest sights is that of a six-year-old dragging a heavy briefcase loaded with homework assignments; not only is this an unhappy task, it is usually a futile one. For we know a young child not only still needs lots of first-hand learning experiences, but also that overburdening beginning readers with formal skills can be disastrous.

So keep a light touch with the "pretend homework." Suggest to your youngster that she:

· make labels
· write a note to a friend—she can dictate it to you, for copying
· dictate a story or a report to you
· dictate a poem for copying
· write her name, her address, and other known words
· illustrate all the above.

This is enough. The aim is to keep her enthusiasm high, her interest vivid. When you see she's getting bored or tired, then stop. Your real reinforcement of new skills comes from your daily sharing of a book.

## Stretching Imagination and Broadening Concepts

One of the innovative teaching methods offered to bright children is asking them to think of all possible meanings of a word. Jasmine Quayle gives us an example of how to enlarge a young child's perception of the meaning of a word:

My six-year-old daughter Eloise was copying the word *tool*.
"Look, Mommy," she said, "here's *too; too* is inside *tool*."
"You're right," I answered. "You've got pretty sharp eyes to see that little word *too* hiding in *tool*."

Then I ventured to expand her concept a little more. "What does *tool* mean?" I asked Eloise.

For a moment she looked baffled, then cried, "Oh, a shovel!"

"Right!" I said. "A shovel is a *tool*. Want to find out what else is a tool?"

Eloise looked doubtful, but I pushed on.

"Let's look in the dictionary!" I suggested. I dragged out the dictionary, saying, "They put the words in alphabetical order. That means all the A words come first, then the B words, then what next?"

"The C's!" shouted Eloise. "The C comes next!"

I was thumbing through the big book. "Where is T?" I asked. "In the front of the alphabet? Near the end of the alphabet?"

Eloise looked at the floor and shrugged her shoulders. I had embarrassed her. She knew the alphabet well enough to race through it at top speed. But she never thought of the letters apart from their alphabet place. I had asked her to think beyond her scope at that time.

"Tell you what," I said. "Help me say the alphabet, and I'll turn the pages that match the letters we say. When we get to T, stop!"

Eloise cheered up and began to recite. Eloise and I reached T in a dead heat. She yelled, "T! Stop!"

I quickly found *TOOL* and read some of the definitions, changing them only slightly so that Eloise could understand.

"*TOOL* . . . for performing . . . doing mechanical operations . . . as a hammer, a saw, . . . anything used as a tool . . . something that helps you do work . . . as . . . a doctor's tools, kitchen tools."

Then I asked, "Can you think of any kitchen tools that help you?"

"Yeah," Eloise answered. "The can opener and the blender."

"How about a knife and fork?" I asked. "Would they help you?"

"Sure," said Eloise, "they help me eat."

"So they are tools, too, aren't they?" I said.

You may think I'm WonderWoman, having all this time to spend with Eloise. Actually, I was helping her get undressed. I work downtown, so early morning and after supper are the only times I have for this kind of special fun; as the man says, it's not the *amount* of time you spend with your kid, it's *how* you spend it.

## Providing Concrete Examples to Make School More Vivid

Many first grade classes often have projects as a basis for developing the language skills of reading and writing, as well as math skills. If your child is engaged in such a project, you may be able to offer additional information in books or by trips. The father of six-year-old Mark gives an example:

Mark's first grade was engaged in a project on Native Americans. When I saw how enthusiastic Mark was, I said, "Indians were supposed to have lived right here, Mark. When the workmen were digging a road through our hill, some of them found old Indian arrowheads."

Mark's eyes widened. "Can we look, too?" he begged. "Please, Daddy?"

How could I resist? So one Saturday he and I went out to the cut where the road was laid. We dug and dug and dug; we found lots of stones, but none looked like arrowheads to me. But Mark wasn't discouraged. Next day he showed up with two classmates, all eager to dig away. This time I got Mark's big sister Lara to take charge of the day. Later, they came whooping back dirty and triumphant, carrying three stones they insisted were arrowheads.

When we went for our weekly library visit, Mark wanted books about arrowheads. Though he couldn't read the text, he examined the pictures eagerly. The librarian told us there were real arrowheads on display at City Hall. City Hall was our next stop. Mark not only found the display exciting, but was thrilled when Joe, the elderly guardian, told him that Joe's grandfather traded with the Indians here.

Oh, on another day we went to the library for books about Indians, which Mark pored over. That night Mark said, "Know what, Daddy? Indian kids liked to play ball just like me!" I really felt then that, for the first time, Mark was seeing these long-ago Indians as fellow human beings.

Mark's father was helping to reinforce his son's classroom theme by outside first-hand and book experiences; he was also helping to enlarge Mark's concepts and sharpen his thinking.

## THE END IS THE BEGINNING

As the school days slip by into school years, the bridging of home and school help in learning to read, and is still strengthened by reading aloud to your child. Some parents may feel this is no longer necessary when their child can read. Isn't the child able to continue on his own now?

Sure. But he is still able to read only easy-to-read books. And even if he has progressed to slightly longer books, he is still in the beginning stages. Think about music: would you stop playing Beethoven because your child can play the scales? or render "The Pixie's Good Night Song" without fumbling?

So it is with reading aloud. Now you both can explore the more difficult books—perhaps the books you enjoyed as a child. For instance, reading E. B. White's *Charlotte's Web* can be an emotional experience not only for the young child but for you and the older children, too.

How else will your child hear the full range of the English language? In what other simple way can he be exposed to the variety of expression and meaning found by listening to some of the classics?

Our everyday speech is fairly limited and mundane. The language heard on television is usually terse and ordinary, because there, the emphasis is on action. And the "street language" that our children are hearing daily is vulgar, to say the least. Of course, the stage and some movies are always a rich source of fine language, but how many shows does a child see?

So home is still the best place for children to enrich their language, to hear the wide varieties of English usage, to be imprinted with its grammatical structure and cadences. And reading aloud is the easiest, most pleasurable—and painless—way to accomplish these desirable aims.

As an eminent librarian has said, "We have to hook children on books." We must catch their attention and interest and flare up their imaginations by reading and reading to them. Kids are surrounded by some powerful distractions: TV, video games, and now computers. These are okay, but TV keeps kids passive; video games are primarily look-and-push; and while computers may offer challenges to the mind, too often they are used as reinforcers for rote learning. And all these instruments are costly, far more expensive than any book or series of books. Books also trigger a child's creative response, stimulate thinking, and demand a child's whole attention. Finally, the child who can really read, who has a rich command of our language, is ready for the unknown challenges of the future.

Thus, at the end, we return to what we said at the beginning: the best help you can give your child, whether he is preparing to read or already has a good grasp of that skill, is to read aloud to him. To read good books, to read regularly, to read what you and your child enjoy, is still the basic way to help enrich your child's own reading.

# Bibliography

## GENERAL REFERENCES

*Activities to Learn By: What to Do With Your Preschooler,* Lillian and Godfrey Frankel. Sterling Publishers, New York, 1974.

*The Alphabet Connection: A Parent's and Teacher's Guide to Beginning Reading and Writing,* Pam Palewicz-Rousseau and Lynda Maderas. Schocken Books, New York, 1979.

*Before the Child Reads,* James L. Hymes, Jr. Harper & Row, New York, 1964.

*Children's Experiences Prior to First Grade and Success in Beginning Reading,* Millie Corinne Almy. Teachers' College, Columbia University, 1949.

*Children's Reading in the Home,* May Hill Arbuthnot. Scott Foresman, Glenview, Ill., 1969.

*Child's Eye View,* Dr. Carol Tomlinson-Keasey. St. Martin's Press, New York, 1980.

*Clear and Lively Writing: Language Games and Activities for Everyone,* Priscilla Vail. Walker, New York, 1981.

*Criteria for the Evaluation of Language Arts Materials in Early Childhood,* Dorothy H. Cohen. Early Childhood Education Council of New York, New York, 1971.

*Don't Push Me, I'm No Computer,* Helen L. Beck. McGraw Hill, New York, 1973.

*Don't Push Your Preschooler,* Louise Bates Ames and Joan Ames Chase. Harper & Row, New York, 1980.

*Effective Teaching of Reading,* Albert J. Harris. David McKay, New York, 1964.

*Give Your Child a Head Start in Reading,* Fitzhugh Dodson, Ph.D. Simon and Schuster, New York, 1981.

*Growing Into Reading,* Marion Monroe. Greenwood Press, Westport, Ct., 1951.

*Home Guide to Early Reading,* Toni S. Gould. Penguin, New York, 1978.

*How to Help Your Child Start School: A Practical Guide for Parents and Teachers of Four to Six Year Olds,* Bernard Ryan, Jr. Perigee Books (Putnam), New York, 1981.

*The Hurried Child,* David Elkind. Addison-Wesley, Reading, Mass., 1981.

*Kindergarten and Early Schooling,* Dorothy Cohen and Marguerita Rudolph. Prentice Hall, Englewood Cliffs, N.J., 1977.

*Language Art: An Idea Book,* Mary Yanaga George. Chandler, Novato, California, 1970.

*The Learning Child,* Dorothy Cohen. Pantheon, New York, 1973.

*Learning for Little Kids,* Sandy Jones. Houghton Mifflin, Boston, 1979.

*Learning Through Play,* Jean Marzolla and Janice Lloyd. Harper Colophon Books, New York, 1972.

*The Pleasure of Their Company: How to Have More Fun with Your Children,* The Bank Street College: Editors Hooks, Boegehold, Reit. Chilton Book Company, Radner, Penn., 1981.

*Preparing Your Child for Reading,* Miles A. Tinker. McGraw Hill, New York, 1971.

*Preparing Your PreSchooler for Reading: A Book of Games,* Brandon Sparkman and Jane Saul. Schocken Books, New York, 1977.

*Psychology and Education: An Introduction,* Jerome Kagan and Cynthia Lang. Harcourt, New York, 1978.

*The Read-Aloud Handbook,* Jim Trelease. Penguin Books, 1982.

*Reading Activities for Child Involvement,* Evelyn B. Spache. Allyn and Bacon, Boston, 1982.

*Reading and Loving,* Leila Berg. Routledge and Kegan Paul, London, 1976.

*The Reading Triangle: Parents Can Help Children Succeed in Reading,* Linda M. Clinard. Focus Publishing Co., Michigan, 1981.

"Schooling Children in a Nasty Climate," Jerome Bruner, *Psychology Today.* January, 1982.

*So Much to Say: How to Help Your Child Learn to Talk,* Edmund Blair Bales. St. Martin's Press, 1982.

*Teach Your Baby,* Dr. Genevieve Painter. Cornerstone Library (Simon & Schuster), New York, 1971, 1982.

*Total Child Care from Birth to Five,* Lorisa DeLorenzo and Robert DeLorenzo. Doubleday, New York, 1982.

*Total Learning for the Whole Child: Holistic Curriculum for Children ages 2 to 5,* Joanne Hendrick. C.V. Mosby Company, St. Louis, Missouri, 1980.

*Understanding Your Child From Birth to Three: A Guide to Your Child's Psychological Development,* Joseph Church. Pocket Books, New York, 1973.

*Young Children Thinking,* Alice Yardley. Citation Press, New York, 1973.

*Your Child Can Read and You Can Help: A Book for Parents,* Dr. Jane Ervin. Doubleday, Garden City, N.Y., 1979.

*Your Child Learns Naturally: What Can You Do to Help Prepare Your Child for School?* Silas L. Warner, M.D., and Edward B. Rosenberg. Doubleday, Garden City, N.Y., 1976.

*Your Three Year Old, Friend or Enemy,* Louise Bates Ames and Frances L. Gesell. Dell Paperbacks, New York, 1980.

*Your Four Year Old, Wild and Wonderful,* Louise Bates Ames

and Frances L. Gesell. A Delta Paperback, Dell, New York, 1976.

*Your Five Year Old, Sunny and Serene,* Louise Bates Ames and Frances L. Gesell. Dell Paperbacks, New York, 1981.

## BOOKS ABOUT CHILDREN'S BOOKS

*The Children's Picture Book: How to Write It. How to Sell It,* Ellen M. Roberts. Writer's Digest Books, Cincinnati, Ohio, 1981.

*Choosing Books for Children: A Commonsense Guide,* Betsy Hearne, Delacorte, New York, 1981.

*A Guide to Non-Sexist Children's Books,* introduction by Alan Alda, compiled by Judith Adell and Hilary Dole Klein. Academy Press Limited, Chicago, 1976.

*A Parent's Guide to Children's Reading,* Nancy Larrick. Westminster Press, Philadelphia, 1982.

*The World of Books for Children: A Parents' Guide,* by Abby Campbell Hunt. Sovereign Books, Simon & Schuster, 1979.

*Writing for Young Children,* Claudia Lewis. Anchor Press, Doubleday, Garden City, N.Y., 1981.

## BOOKS RELATED TO TELEVISION

*The Family Guide to Children's Television: What to Watch, What to Miss, What to Change and How to Do It,* Evelyn Kaye. Pantheon Books, New York, 1974.

*New Season: The Positive Use of Commercial Television With Children,* Rosemary Lee Patten. Charles E. Merrill Publishing Co., Columbus, Ohio, 1976.

*Partners in Play,* Dorothy G. Singer and Jerome L. Singer. Harper & Row, New York, 1978.

*The Show and Tell Machine: How Television Works and Works You Over,* Rose K. Goldsen. A Delta Paperback, Dell, New York, 1978.

*Television: How to Use it Wisely with Children,* Child Study Association, Josette Frank, Ed. The Child Study Press, New York, 1976.

*Television and the Preschool Child,* Harvey Lesser. Academic Press, New York, 1979.

*TV On/Off: Better Use of Family Television,* Ellen B. De-Franco. Goodyear Paperback, Santa Monica, Calif., 1980.

# Index